THE
HIMALAYAS

SMITHMARK

Contents

Text by
Marco Majrani

Edited by
Valeria Manferto

Designed by
Patrizia Balocco

1 *This painting is in the* gompa *(monastery) of Spituk, in Ladakh. The "Wheel of Life" is perhaps the most common image in the iconography of the Buddhist world. Photograph by Jaroslav Poncar / Bruce Coleman.*

2-3 *The daunting south wall of Lhotse, which stands in Nepal, reaches an altitude of 8501 meters. Photograph by Toru Nakano / Agence Freestyle.*

4-5 *Ama Dablam (6856 meters), a sacred mountain of great beauty, rears up over the monastery of Thyangboche, which stands in the Nepalese valley of Khumbu. Photograph by Pat Morrow / First Light.*

6-7 *The slopes of Z3 in Zanskar, are shrouded by the early evening shadows. Photograph by Marco Majrani.*

8 *A Tibetan pilgrim prays before the Kailas, a sacred and inviolable peak, the center of the Universe for both Buddhists and Hindus. Photograph by Galen Rowell / Mountain Light.*

9 *Nuptse, a mountain that rises 7879 meters above sea level, is in Nepal, in the region around Everest. Photograph by Christophe Boisvieux.*

10-11 *The rainbow seems to come to earth directly over the great palace of Potala in Lhasa, Tibet. Photograph by Galen Rowell / Mountain Light.*

12-13 *A thangka, or silk tapestry with a religious subject, is displayed during the festival of Tchasho in the temple of Wangdi Phodan, in Bhutan. Photograph by Nazima Kowall.*

© 1994 Edizioni White Star
Via Candido Sassone, 24
13100 Vercelli, Italy

This edition distributed in U.S.A. and Canada by SMITHMARK Publishers Inc;
16 East 32nd Street ,
New York, NY 10016
Tel. (212) 532-6600

SMITHMARK books are available for bulk purchase for sales promotion and premium use. For details write or call the Manager of Special Sales, SMITHMARK Publishers Inc., 16 East 32nd Street, New York, NY 10016; (212)532-6600

0-8317-8682-5

Printed in Italy by Canale, Torino.

THE HIMALAYAS
ABODE OF THE GODS

The Himalayas are a world unto themselves. Here, in the "Home of the Snows", time and space have meanings unlike anything that we have come to know elsewhere. The Himalayas are one of those places that it is impossible to describe; sensations and feelings, impressions and terrors here come hard on the heels of each other, mingling in confusion as in a dream; reality and fantasy overlap, each concealing the identity of the other. One must have been born amidst these mountains, or live here at length, if one is to grasp the subtle and inscrutable nuances that permeate the essence of everything. Any attempt to define this region, any phrase, any adjective inevitably proves incomplete, inadequate to the vast subject at hand. Here all is grandeur, measureless, majestic, and shrouded in mystery, everything is at once terrifying and alluring, sublime and deadly mortal. In the Himalayas, at times that which may seem fantastic and unreal proves far more solid than that which meets the eye. On every side one feels the presence of arcane and unsettling beings, of spirits that are at time benevolent and at others hostile, in the most surprising of settings that the human mind can conceive of, amidst icy silences broken only by the dull roar of avalanches, by the metallic rattle and ping of the ices, and by the intermittent hiss of the winds. The mountains are considered to be the altars of the gods, and as such they are sacred. Some of those mountains are considered inviolable, because the mere presence of humans cannot taint the home of mighty deities; we shall speak of these mountains at some greater length in later chapters. The Tibetan and Sanskrit names of the mountains often remind us of the fact that these peaks are something more than a crystallized mass of rocks and minerals. Just to mention a few names, Chomo Lungma, the Tibetan name for Everest, means "Land of the Goddess, Mother of the Earth"; Cho Oyu means "Buttress of Faith"; Manaslu means "Mountain of the Spirit"; Gosainthan, the Sanskrit name for Shisha Pangma, means "Place of the Holy"; Khan Tengri means the "Lord of Spirits"; and Annapurna means "Goddess of Bountiful Harvests". In the Tibetan highlands, in the green ocean of the deepest valleys of Nepal, in the cold and arid expanses of Ladakh and Zanskar, in the blinding and eternal glitter of the snows on the highest and most unattainable of peaks, one never feels alone. Giuseppe Tucci, the leading scholar of the Far East in Italy, who had the opportunity and the courage to explore this region on foot as early as the Thirties and Forties, wrote the following about the immense and desolate expanses of Tibet and the steep slopes of the profound valleys: "The solitude is not empty here; indeed, it teems with life. The appropriate rite and formulas are the talisman of the wayfarer. If the presences are favorable to him, then he has nothing to fear: raging rivers, rockslides, and avalanches will not touch him. When he is hungry, he will find someone who will give him food." To a Tibetan, if climbing to considerable heights causes dizziness, this is not because of any shortage of oxygen, but because of the influence of malign spirits or because the spirit of the wayfarer is not powerful enough. When a Tibetan makes a pilgrimage or a simple trip, he is not driven by curiosity about other peoples, other places, or other faces of nature.

The beauties of the landscape or of art do not interest him, a thousand things that we Westerners admire and observe are of no interest to him, because he looks within, because he meditates and prays. What counts for a Tibetan is chiefly the soul; a monastery is not considered to be more or less interesting because of its architecture or the works of art that are contained within it, but because of the greater or lesser sacredness of the place in which that monastery is built. Every place is sacred, because God is everywhere. When the way is difficult and dangerous, instead of improving the roadway itself, the Tibetans choose to carve prayers into the rocks, convinced that in this way, good will triumph over evil. Prayer and meditation thus merge with a serene and fatalistic vision of existence. There is a motto that goes: "Kneel where others have knelt, because God is present where many have prayed." And so, along the paths and trails, the presence of the supernatural is marked by unending clues and indications, as if an invisible network of spiritual routes overlapped the real itineraries of the mountains. It is enough to take a trip through the

15 Light seems to play along the dizzying wall of Gangapurna and it highlights the remarkable formations of snow and ice, usually described as "organ-pipe" formations. This mountain, which rises 7455 meters above sea level, is part of the Annapurna group, a system of huge massifs that tower above the level of seven thousand meters, and which form a distinctive part of the majestic panorama of the high Himalayas in the Manang district, in Nepal. The runoff from Gangapurna, moreover, with a full-fledged cascade of seracs, feeds a glittering glacial lake. Photograph by Galen Rowell / Mountain Light.

16 *Tibetan religious art manifests itself in all its richness in the fresco shown in the photograph, which is preserved in the ancient monastery of Hemis. This* gompa, *built at the beginning of the seventeenth century at Leh, capital of Ladakh, contains a noteworthy gallery of wall paintings.*

The composition of these sacred images adheres to well established rules; nonetheless, even though it is necessary to respect certain formal conditions, the rigid form offers infinite variations in color and composition. Photograph by Marcello Bertinetti.

17 *In the monastery of Shey, in Ladakh, a giant statue of the Buddha in the shade seems to observe with a peaceful gaze a second statue of a praying Buddha. The hands of the god, who is seated in the typical lotus position, have a great symbolic value, and - depending on the direction in which they are pointing - indicate the general attitude of the Buddha toward humankind. When the Buddha's hands are joined in his lap, it means that the god is meditating. When the left hand is in* the Buddha's lap and the right hand rests on his knee, pointing downward, with the back of the hand facing upward, then the deity is demonstrating a wish to touch the earth and to be close to it. When the palm of the right hand faces upward, it means that the Buddha is expressing solidarity with human suffering and compassion. And when the right hand is raised and the palm is facing outward, it emphasizes the Buddha's courage. Photograph by Marcello Bertinetti.*

valley of Ladakh or Nepal in order to see how the world of the Himalayas presents us with the most imaginative series of "utensils of prayer" that the human mind has ever invented: the range is vast, and includes chorten *and little* stupa, *the architecture of which symbolizes the cosmos and the planet, and which we could consider in much the same role as our little mountain votive chapels, also serving as indicators and signposts;* mani walls, *made up of hundreds or thousands of stones, carved with bas-reliefs or sculptures by wayfarers, and then abandoned along the mountain paths; prayer wheels, little spinning fans upon which mantras are written;* tarch , *little silk and paper banners that flutter at the tip of tall wooden poles, or tied to long cords like so much washing hung out to dry, launching the sacred inscriptions they bear out into the winds;* thangkas, *silken drapes that depict the sacred elements;* mandalas, *the formulas for meditation depicted on the "wheel of life". In particular, the prayer wheels can be of various sorts - giant cylinders that are made to spin through the concerted efforts of a number of individuals; cylinders that rotate through the power of water, wind, or tiny currents of warm air that rise from lanterns or chimneys; or else tiny portable cylinders with a handle and a sphere made of wood, bone, or silver, which serves as the counterweight for spinning by hand. The* chorten, *which are present everywhere, especially at high passes and in the most difficult or dangerous points of the trails, are reliquaries, conical in shape, only a few meters in height, whose architecture symbolizes the cosmos and our planet. The base represents the earth; the hemispherical section, or "pot", symbolizes water; the conical part, made up of thirteen stacked components, represents fire; the crescent moon that stands above it all is a symbol of air; and the uppermost sphere, or "sun", amounts to the idea of space as an elevated and unattainable entity. One must always walk around the* chorten *in a clockwise direction (only the followers of the ancient religion of Bon-po walk in the opposite direction). Likewise, one must walk past the* mani walls *along the left-hand side. When walking around a* chorten *or walking along a* mani wall, *the wayfarer will automatically recite all of the invocations that they*

bear. The most common mantra, which is written everywhere, and which is recited during all religious ceremonies, is the famous Sanskrit chant, "Om mani padme hum", which translates literally as: "Hail, o jewel (Buddha) in the lotus flower (the world)". This translation is, however, quite approximate, as it does not take into count the first and the last syllables, Om and Hum. Om is the seed-syllable of the universe, and as it vibrated it created the universe out of chaos; Hum may come from the Sanskrit hu, which means "to sacrifice", and indicates sacrifice as the mission of man upon earth. The magic of this mantra, which the Tibetans claim was dictated directly by God, lies in a great series of hidden meanings. Most people do not know the full significance of this chant, but they recite it with great devotion. That which matters, in fact, is faith, the level of concentration that is attained in pronouncing the mantra.

We find the syllable Om in a great many yoga exercises, as a means of inducing the correct rhythm of breathing and to obtain control over one's body. The profound and intrinsic musicality of this syllable and of the mantra as a whole is effective chiefly because of the "vibrations" that it transmits. It may seem improbable, but lamas - the holiest of the priests - and the yogi and sadhu manage to obtain from their bodies and from their minds remarkable levels of performance, through the correct and repeated recitation of the mantra.

For example, certain Tibetan ascetics, known as Lump , customarily run all the way around the lake of Manasarovar, which lies at an altitude of four thousand meters, near Mount Kailas, running seventy kilometers in a state of trance, or else survive partially naked for months in a cave, at twenty degrees Celsius below zero, through the practice of tum-mo yoga, which is a method of heat conservation that is now used in modern biofeedback training. The scientific study of many phenomena with which we are not familiar, and which Tibetans take for granted, is yielding a great many surprises. For a long time, Westerners smiled indulgently upon Eastern medicine, yoga, and many other religious practices, writing them off as examples of superstition and magic practiced by con-men with cunning sleight-of-hand. We should bear in mind, however, that as

19 top *A group of Gelugpa monks, of the reformed sect of the "Yellow Hats" are blowing their distinctive horns during the Saga Dawa, a festival which takes place in the Tsuklakhang Royal Chapel in the Chogyal Palace, in Gangtok. This city, the capital of the Indian province of Sikkim, is situated at an altitude of over 1500 meters, facing the Kangchenj··nga. The mountain is considered to be the home of the deity of the same name, often shown riding astride a puma, his face dyed red and his head adorned with a crown of five skulls. Legend has it that the god long ago buried five treasures at the top of the mountain: sacred books, precious stones, an impenetrable suit of armor, salt, and medicine. Photograph by Nazima Kowall.*

19 bottom *This picture shows a religious ceremony taking place in the monastery of Rumtek, in Sikkim, in one of the places most sacred to Lamaistic Buddhism. The monastery, located a few kilometers away from Gangtok, and built during the Sixties, is a copy of a Tibetan temple destroyed during the Chinese invasion; it belongs to the reformed sect of the Karmapa "Yellow Hats", a branch founded in the fifteenth century, belonging to the category of Tantric Buddhism. This is a religious school based on the rites contained in the tantras, books which contain magic formulas that allow humans to attain salvation rapidly. Photograph by Earl Kowall.*

20 *The village of
Dharapani, set at the foot
of Dhaulagiri, in north-
central Nepal, practically
along the Tibetan border,
is distinguished by the
houses painted two colors,
and which stand two
storeys tall. The imposing*
*massif of Dhaulagiri,
whose name means
"White Mountain," rises
to an altitude of 8167
meters above sea level, and
dominates all of the
surrounding valleys.
Photograph by
Pat Morrow.*

21 *The natural features
of the Himalayas are harsh
and unforgiving, due to
the altitude and climate,
but the place is also rich
and generous, and the
Nepalese have found no
difficulties in taking from
it all that they need for
their survival. On the
numerous hills of the
province of Pokhara in
Nepal, grain is cultivated
on land made level by
terracing; corn and*

*early as the year 1200 the Codices of the Tibetan
monasteries bore detailed anatomical charts, with
indications concerning the operation of blood
vessels and nerves, while the discovery of the
circulation of blood in western medicine dates
from 1629. The region's pharmacopeia, as well,
based on the healing properties of over fifteen
hundred medicinal herbs, is of considerable
interest and unquestioned efficacy. As of this
writing, western science is beginning to examine -
without blinders - this ancient body of knowledge
which has always placed a great emphasis upon
spirituality as opposed to materialism. Perhaps it
is also as a product of this cultural tradition that
one is seized by doubts in the Himalayas as in no
other place in the world, which is why there is a
clear tendency towards abandonment and
contemplation, and why one feels the presence of
undefinable energies. In places like this, one can
clearly understand how popular legends and
myths, such as that of the yeti, the fantastic
creature - half-man and half-ape - that
supposedly lives in the furthest valleys, along the
snow line, or that of Shangri-La, where time runs
more slowly than it does in the rest of the world,
have found believers. Many call this the "kingdom
of diversity". For a westerner, it is very difficult,
if not actually impossible, to succeed in analyzing
and understanding the profound meaning of the
philosophy of these peoples. Their mentality is too
distant, the pace of their lives is too alien, and
even the grandiose and savage physical environment
is too unlike what we know - this environment is
surely the prime source of inspiration for any and
all internal and external manifestations of their
religious feelings. While for a westerner, the normal
activities of one's everyday routines may be
temporarily interrupted by moments of prayer, for
Tibetans things work in precisely the opposite way -
prayer occupies every moment of the day:
conversations and other normal tasks from time to
time interrupt what would otherwise be a life of
incessant prayer. From a strictly geographic point
of view, the boundaries of the Himalayan region
are defined by the course of the Indus river to the
west, and by that of the Tsang-po to the north and
east, where the river is called the Brahmaputra.
The cultural boundaries of the region are far more*

*vast, however, and they include areas of the Tibetan
highlands to the north of the Tsang-po, which are
inhabited by peoples who fit into the context of the
Buddhist and Lamaist tradition. And this book
takes those ethnic and cultural boundaries as its
frame of reference. To the west of the Indus,
instead, the division is not merely geological and
geographic; this also marks a concrete border with
the world of Islam, which is currently exerting a
powerful penetration into the region, under the
demographic pressure of a burgeoning population.
The peoples of the Himalayas seem to have
developed a series of physiological adaptations to
life in so extreme an environment. They live at
great altitudes, temperatures vary greatly, and
the topography is extremely sheer and rocky.
The inhabitants of "the rooftop of the world" are
distinguished, among other things, by their
amazing strength and stamina, their ability to
carry unbelievable weights on their head and
spinal column, their predominantly vegetarian
diet, and their stout resistance to cold and
exhaustion. They are accustomed to breathing
very thin air, in which the pressure of oxygen may
be as little as half what it would be at sea level -
some permanent settlements may be as high as five
thousand meters above sea level, or even higher -
and as a result there is a different structure of both*

*potatoes are planted as
well, and so the harvests
take place at various
periods throughout the
year. The houses that can
be seen on the slopes are not
permanent residences, but
rather seasonal
habitations, used in the
cultivation of the fields.
In the background,
wrapped in the morning
haze, is the silhouette of
Machapuchare, which rises
to an altitude of 6994
meters; its name means
"Fishtail". Machapuchare
is a sacred and inviolable
mountain, inasmuch as it
is considered to be a
residence of the gods.
In 1957, authorization
was issued to an English
expedition to climb it, on
the understanding that the
climbers halt at least fifty
meters beneath the peak, in
order to keep the mountain
from being defiled, a
condition which was
respected under the
vigilant eyes of the people
from the surrounding
villages.
Photograph by
Pat Morrow/First Light.*

21

rib cage and lung, as well as a larger and sturdier heart. Among the various peoples of the Himalayas, the Sherpas of Nepal are in every way the best adapted, and as a consequence the Sherpas are most sought after as guides for the various expeditions. And it is the proliferation of western expeditions that poses the most serious threat to the conservation of the Himalayan environment. Over recent years, a great many organizations dedicated to the protection of the environment have sent expeditions with the sole and specific purpose of "scouring" the walls of Everest and other peaks from the refuse left behind by hundreds and hundreds of teams of mountain climbers. The arrival of mountain climbers and trekkers en masse has disturbed the fragile economic ties that governed the tranquil lives in the mountain communities. The recent appearance of cavities in the teeth of Nepalese children is certainly due to the candies and chocolates brought by Westerners. At times, so innocent an action as giving candy to a child can lead to unforeseen and undesired consequences. The Himalayan region is an amazing crucible of varied cultures, peoples, and traditions, which have coexisted for centuries in peace and tranquillity, with great and reciprocal respect and tolerance. These peoples basically form part of two major philosophical and religious groups, the Buddhists and the Hindus, both present ever since the eighth century, and only in recent times threatened in any serious way by Islamic fundamentalists and by Chinese aggression, which has been responsible for genocidal devastation in Tibet. Buddhism has taken root, basically, at both ends of the chain, to the west in Ladakh, Spiti, and Lahaul, and to the east in Bhutan, Sikkim, and in the Darjeeling region, as well as in a few of the further and northernmost sections of Nepal, in the Mustang and in the Dolpo regions. Hinduism, on the other hand, is present chiefly in the Indian Himalayan regions of the Punjab and Garhwal, and in Nepal, where it coexists very peacefully with Buddhism. The philosophical and religious appeal is felt so profoundly that in every family in Ladakh or Tibet, at least one member dedicates their life to monkhood. The center of the two religious universes, the so-called "Father and Very Center of the Universe" is perceived to be the sacred mountain Kailas, the "Crystal" where both the Indus and the Tsang-po rivers have their source. "Not even in a hundred ages of the Gods could I tell you of the glories of the Himalayas"; thus reads one of the Puranas, collections of ancient stories that represent one of the great literary works of Hinduism. Rivers of words have been lavished to explain what many consider to be one of the great mysteries of the earth, while in this book we have relied chiefly upon the remarkable efficacy of pictures, which can recreate better than any other tool the emotions that can be given only by an in-depth and direct contact with the places in question, as a confirmation of the principle according to which "a thing that you experience is worth more than a hundred things you have heard".

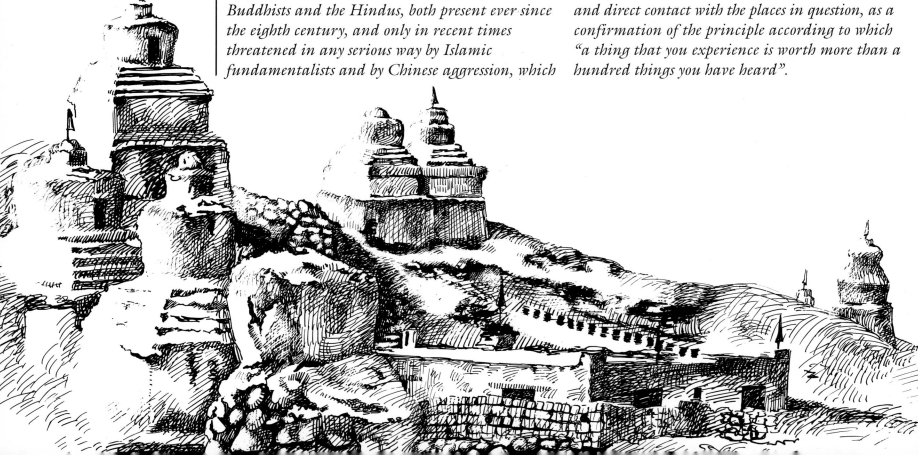

23 *The monastery of Punakha, which was built in 1637, was the winter residence of the king of Bhutan until 1955. This small kingdom opened its borders to visitors only in the last few years. This is the most archaic and feudal portion of the Tibetan world. In Bhutan,* numerous monasteries survive, called dzong, *and the sense of religion is deep-seated and powerful. From a political point of view, the kingdom is closely tied to the mighty and nearby India. Tourism is strictly regulated, and there is a limitation to the number of visitors allowed. The numbers are established personally by the sovereign, in order to prevent excessive modifications in the delicate economic structure, essentially agrarian and pastoral in nature.*
Photograph by Earl Kowall.

24-25 *The children shown in this picture have a rather remarkable schoolroom: the wide-open outdoors at the foot of the Himalayan range, near Stok, in Ladakh.*
Photograph by Earl Kowall.

26-27 *In winter, many of the villages in Zanskar remain isolated for six to eight months of the year, caught in a clamp of snow and ice.*
Photograph by Olivier Föllmi.

28-29 *The source of the Ganges, which is in Uttar Pradesh, is one of the holiest places in the Hindu religion.*
Photograph by Marcello Bertinetti.

WHERE THE MOUNTAINS DANGLE FROM THE SKY

*T*he Himalayas are far
and away the most significant chain of
mountains in the world. The chain extends for
twenty-five hundred kilometers, joining to the
west and the northwest with the mountain chains
of the Karakorum and the Hindu Kush, which
are geologically distinct but are also joined to the
principal chain. In total, including the outlying
chains, this system of mountains contains all
fourteen of the world's mountain peaks that tower
above eight thousand meters, as well as seventy-
five peaks that top seven thousand meters, and one
hundred fourteen peaks taller than six thousand
meters. Many of these peaks, if we exclude the
principal ones, have not yet been scaled, and some
have not yet even been named, a number of valleys
have not yet been explored, as incredible as that
may seem on the eve of the twenty-first century.
The inviolability of some of these peaks may be
laid to religious reasons, and not because they are
particularly difficult in technical terms - such is
the case with Kailas, Machapuchare,
Kangchenjunga, Ama Dablam, Gauri Shankar,
Shivling, and other mountains still; for the most
part, the government agencies in question bow to
the wishes of the religious authorities and local
communities, and do not issue climbing permits.
Save for a very few exceptions, it has only been
over the past few decades that the Himalayan
region has to any real extent opened its doors to
Western scientists and explorers, and the Tibetan
area, occupied by the Chinese invaders, has only
been accessible since 1980. These factors have led
to an overall delay in the study of this portion of
our planet, as interesting as the area may be and
as numerous and complex as may be the changes
through which it is constantly being ushered.
For this reason, alongside the remarkable feats of
extreme mountain climbing to which this region
is often witness, there are increasingly frequent
expeditions engaged in research and exploration.
Scholars and scientists, who can study the most
spectacular and grandiose phenomena of geology
in this area, do not conceal their excitement, and
yet there remains considerable leeway on the
interpretation of the data. Scientific
interpretations, therefore, are open to revision;
nonetheless there seems to be a certain degree of
unanimity of opinion, in part thanks to the

30-31 *The warm light of
the sunset seems to play
along the slopes of
Machapuchare in the
Annapurna group,
creating a dreamscape
which emphasizes the
sacred nature of the
mountain, believed to be
the sacred home of gods.
Indeed, the inhabitants of
Nepal claim that their
gods live amongst the
mountains, and - under
the influence of alluring
shapes and colors - their
beliefs start to seem quite
credible to Western eyes as
well.
Photograph by
Marco Majrani.*

development of the techniques of seismological, paleomagnetic, and radiometric research. The overall phenomenon should be set in the context of the theory of tectonic plates. The geological history of our planet provides an unending source of amazement even to the scholars in this field. Suffice it to consider the fact that on some of the highest peaks of the Himalayas, and even on the highest tips of Everest and Annapurna, it is possible to detect clearly the unmistakable traces of a past spent at the bottom of the ocean. Indeed, amidst the rocky strata located at over eight thousand meters of elevation, it is quite common to find fossil remains that once formed the bodies of marine creatures. This means that the very formations that once constituted the deepest of seabeds must have undergone powerful up-thrusts that drove them as far as ten or twelve thousand meters straight into the air. If we are to understand the processes that led to the creation of the Himalayan mountain chain, we must first describe the fundamental components of the theory of plate tectonics, according to which the earth's crust is divided up into a dozen continental plates capable of shifting slowly one with respect to another, like huge rafts on an ocean. The "engine" driving this movement should be sought in the layer lying immediately beneath the crust, known as the mantle, which is the site of continuous subductive movements (not unlike the motion that occurs in a pot of oatmeal on a slow boil); the velocity of these movements can be estimated at about five to six centimeters per year. The shifting of the continental plates at times result in enormous collisions, during which the edges of the plates crumple and "accordion" like the sheet metal of two automobiles in a crash. Just a few centimeters a year of velocity may not seem like much at the speed at which human lives are lived, but in comparison with the speed of geology, they correspond to shifts of thousands of kilometers over the course of dozens of millions of years, as in the case that led to the creation of the Himalayas. Indeed, the subcontinent of India was once a great island, floating free from what is now Antarctica and Southern Africa. Over the last seventy-five million years, India has traveled over five thousand kilometers, moving in a north-easterly direction, until it finally crashed into the Eurasian continent.

36 *The last rays of sunlight seem to want to linger on the peaks of Everest and the Chinese mountain of Changtse (7553 meters). In the foreground, one may note a number of tall ice pinnacles that line the* slopes of the tallest mountain on the planet. For glaciologists, the manner in which these pinnacles form is still the subject of study and speculation. *Photograph by Pascal Tournaire.*

37 top *The light that plays along the walls of Everest, with the glittering reflections from the snow, seems to emerge from the mountain itself; indeed, the Tibetans say that "the bird that flies over the peak of Everest goes blind." Photograph by Pascal Tournaire.*

36-37 *From Kala Pattar, the "Black Mountain," one enjoys a breath-taking view of the majestic pyramid of Everest. The tallest peak on earth is called* Chomo Lungma, *"Mother Goddess of All the Snows"; in Nepal, on the other hand, her name is* Sagarmatha, *"Head of the Ocean." Photograph by Pat Morrow / First Light.*

38-39 *The remarkable serac of the ice fall on Everest represents an obligatory passage for all mountain climbers who want to reach the South Col, the pass between the peaks of Everest and Lhotse.*
Photograph by Pascal Tournaire.

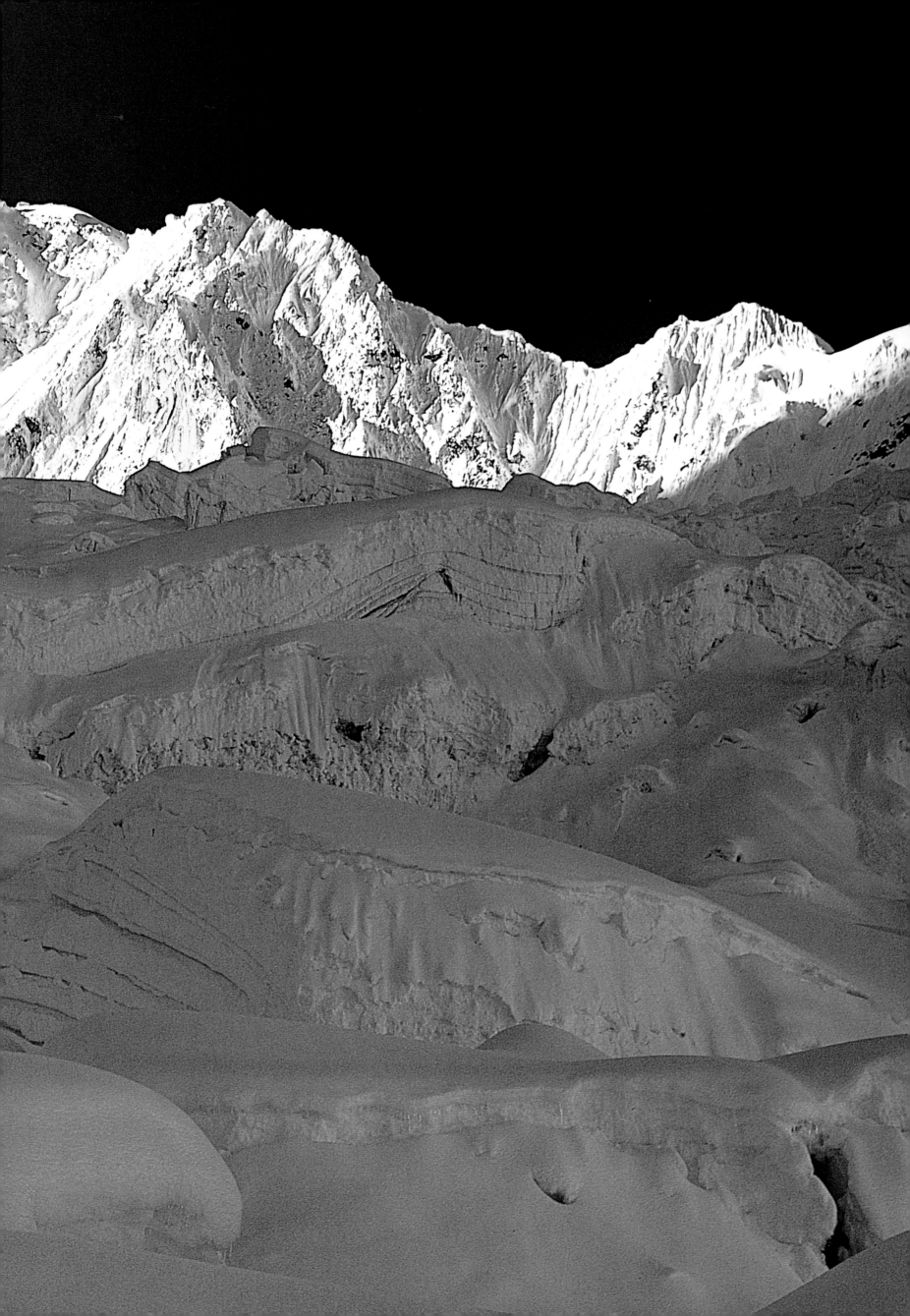

40 *This photograph, taken at dawn from the west face of Everest, helps us to form some idea of the vastness of the Himalayas. To the left, in fact, the sun is already lighting up the snowy expanses hemmed in by cloudbanks while, to the right, the valleys of Rongbuk, toward which the tongue of the glacier points downward, are still wrapped in the total darkness of night. In the background, an eight-thousand-meter peak rears up, Cho Oyu, considered a fairly easy climb at 8157 meters; the name means "Goddess of Turquoise". Photograph by Pascal Tournaire.*

*41 There are a great
many obligatory passages
for those who undertake to
climb Everest. In this
picture, it is possible to
admire the valley that
leads to the ice fall,
between Everest and
Nuptse, as seen from the
advanced base camp.
Photograph by
Pascal Tournaire.*

*42-43 The face of
Nuptse is enveloped in
threatening clouds, which
partly conceal the eternal
snows. This photograph
was taken during a climb
to an altitude of more
than six thousand meters.
Photograph by
Pascal Tournaire.*

*44-45 Once again,
nature astounds and
surprises. The two figures
below reveal the impotence
of humans in comparison
with the mighty South Face
of Nuptse which, in the
evening twilight, is
marked by a surreal welter
of cuts in the sheer face.
Photograph by Pat Morrow.*

The effect of the enormous collision, which began some forty million years ago, and which has not yet exhausted all its enormous energy, was the creation of the most imposing mountain range on the planet. From when the collision began, India has continued to move northward some two thousand kilometers more, producing a remarkable thickening of the earth's crust. The rise of the Alps, too, is approximately simultaneous with that of the Himalayas, and fits into the same class of phenomena. Geologists generally speak of "the Alpine-Himalayan orogenetic cycle," classing the Alps, Carpathians, Caucasus, Alborz, Hindu Kush, Karakorum, and Himalayas together, as if they were practically a single chain. The traces of the closure of the ocean that once divided India from Eurasia can thus be found in the high valleys of the Indus and the Tsang-po, along a line that can clearly be seen in satellite photographs, and which has been given the name of the "Indus-Tsang-po suture," and along the highest peaks, as hems of the continental seabed "wrung out" and hung up to dry, so to speak. As a consequence of this colossal collision, the earth's crust in this region has been shortened by a good three hundred kilometers, and its thickness has increased to as much as seventy kilometers, greater than anywhere else on the planet. The impact has not yet exhausted itself, and the mountain chain continues to grow, as we can see from the morphology of the jagged sharp peaks and the deep valleys, although erosion is very intense, especially in the southern regions, where precipitation in general is the heaviest. This means that erosion, although it is very intense, cannot outpace the continuous upthrust. The climate of the Himalayan region features distinctive geographic and seasonal contrasts, a function of the existence of the monsoon, a hot damp wind that blows along the mountain slopes, originating in the Indian Ocean. It is no accident that the word "monsoon" comes from the Arabic word mausin, which means season. During the summer, the Himalayas are affected by this atmospheric flow, which generates violent and frequent rainstorms, especially along the southern slopes and the eastern sections of the mountain chain. The intensity of the phenomena decreases as one moves northward, and ceases almost entirely in the Tibetan region. Cherrapunji, a town situated in Meghalaya, at an altitude of 1310

meters, amidst the pre-Himalayan hills, is the rainiest place in the world, with an average annual rainfall of 12,040 millimeters, and a record annual rainfall of 26,460 millimeters. In Kathmandu, about seven hundred kilometers to the west, the average annual rainfall drops to 1,350 millimeters and at Leh, in the heart of Ladakh, only 85 millimeters of rain falls every year. In the area around Tibet, the infrequent precipitation is almost exclusively limited to winter snowfall. The elevated rainfall leads to the formation of extensive glacial basins, the largest in the world outside of the polar regions. Considering that these are sub-tropical latitudes, the temperatures are appropriate to the altitude, although there are extreme thermal variations according to the season and to the time of day in the western desert regions. In summer, in the Indus Valley, it is common to exceed temperatures of 50 degrees Celsius in the shade, while during winter in the same areas the mercury drops to minus 20 degrees Celsius, and the level of the perennial snowline is at about 4800 meters. In Ladakh and in Chinese Tibet, too, we find similar conditions, but because of the great elevation - on average greater than thirty-five hundred meters, temperatures approach 30 degrees Celsius during the summer, and in the winter may drop below 40 degrees Celsius below zero, with annual temperature ranges spanning more than 70 degrees Celsius! In the arid and cold region of Drass, near Leh, just beyond the pass that marks the western boundary of Ladakh, temperatures of minus 58 degrees Celsius have been recorded. In Nepal, the climate is less extreme, especially because of the abundance of precipitation and the more forested environment. The snow line is at 5500 meters. At Kathmandu the average temperature in January is 10.2 degrees Celsius, while the average temperature in July is 24.5 degrees Celsius. If one wishes to plan a trip to the Himalayas, it is essential to be familiar with the climate. The best months are those before or after the monsoons, which is to say, April-May, and October-November. Non-climbers can go to Nepal even in winter, and be certain that they will find splendid clear skies, while in that period it is far more risky to climb because of the jet streams, typical of the Himalayan latitudes. At altitudes of eight thousand meters, these winds can be faster than 250 kilometers per hour and be as cold as 70 degrees Celsius below zero.

47 The slopes of Nilgiri, which soars to an altitude of 7032 meters above sea level, jut from the dim light to stand in all their magnificent splendor. This mountain, of which we can see the south face, stands in the Nepalese Himalayas, a predominantly mountainous area that attracts a great many climbers. Here there are dozens of mountains that stand over seven thousand meters high, and a great many of these peaks have never been scaled. Photograph by Galen Rowell / Mountain Light.

48-49 Lhotse, the fourth-highest mountain in the world, stands in the Khumbu region, in Nepal. It is the largest satellite peak of Everest, and it is often unfairly overlooked because of its proximity to the tallest mountain on earth. In this picture, we can clearly see signs of the stratification of ancient ocean sediments: what was once several thousand meters under the surface of the sea now towers at eight thousand meters above sea level. Photograph by Pat Morrow / First Light.

46

50 top *Tserim Kang, towering 6935 meters above sea level, is one of the most incredible and intriguing mountains in Bhutan. This country, which is called* Druk Yul *in Bhutanese, meaning "the Land of the Dragon", lies in the eastern section of the Himalayan chain, and to north is riven by mountains soaring above seven thousand meters. Photograph by Earl Kowall.*

50-51 *Although this is one of the "lesser" peaks of the Annapurna group, Hiunchuli rears up into the thin air, reaching an altitude of 6441 meters. The photograph, which deftly emphasizes the glittering white of the permanent snows, was shot from the base camp of the "Sanctuary". Photograph by Pascal Tournaire.*

51 right *Nepal's largely mountainous Khumbu region features two other "sleeping giants" - Kang Tega, which stands 6779 meters in altitude, and can be seen on the left in the photograph, and Tramserku, on the right, which towers above 6600 meters. Photograph by Pat Morrow / First Light.*

52-53 *Kangchenjunga means "The Five Strongboxes of the Great Snows" in Tibetan. This peak, with its mighty bulk rising 8597 meters above sea level, constitutes a massive wall straddling the land between Nepal and Sikkim, and is the third tallest mountain on the planet. It is a sacred peak, and mountain climbers are obliged to stop climbing just a few meters below the peak in order to keep from defiling it. Photograph by Nazima Kowall.*

55 *The imposing bulk of Cholatse, a Nepalese mountain that stands in the Khumbu region, glitters in the reflected light of the last rays of sunlight, which emphasize* *the harmonious shapes of the snow. This mountain, which is also known as Jobo Lhaptshan, is 6440 meters in height. Photograph by Galen Rowell / Mountain Light.*

Chinese Tibet and Ladakh are not affected by the monsoons, and so it is possible to visit them with a view to mountain climbing all summer, while they are cold in the winter and almost impracticable due to the closure of the passes that normally provide access. The difficulty of traveling through the Himalayan region due to the extreme climate, the elevated altitude of the passes, and their frequent blockage, has always constituted a major obstacle to communications and exploration. Nonetheless, even before the times of Marco Polo, merchants and adventurers made their way to these distant lands, attracted by the wealth that was concealed, or that they believed was hidden here. If we leave aside Marco Polo, who did no more than to travel around the mountain chain, the first Europeans to penetrate to the heart of the Himalayas via the Mana Pass, reaching the town of Tsaparang, were the Jesuit fathers Antonio de Andrade and Manuel Marques, in June 1624. For more than a century, no one but Jesuit missionaries came to the region, among them Father Ippolito Desideri, who reached Lhasa in 1714, where he lived for five years, studying in depth the Lamaistic religion. In 1735, an atlas published in Paris by the geographer Jean-Baptiste d'Anville showed, for the first time, the existence of Everest, with the Sanskrit name of Chomo Lungma. In 1811, disguised as fakirs, William Moorcroft and Hyder Young Hearsey reached the sacred lake of Manasarovar, and explored Ladakh.

The region was, for years, a throughway for a number of varieties of commerce: that of salt, silk, wool, spices, metals, and precious stones, which were transported from Persia and India to China, and vice versa. Lands like Ladakh were considered an obligatory part of the route, and it is no accident that the very name Ladakh means "Land of Mountain Passes". Even today, long caravans of yaks, the extremely sturdy local bovines, make their way to altitudes of six thousand meters, going beyond the Tibetan borders, even though the chief use to which these extremely precious animals are put now is that of transporting equipment for mountain climbing expeditions.

During the English rule, the Survey of India was undertaken in 1818, an organization charged with the geographic and geodetic survey of the country. Sir George Everest ran the office from 1830 until 1843, providing a crucial contribution

56-57 Lhotse, which rears to the unbelievable height of 8516 meters, is the most important satellite peak of Everest, divided from that mountain only by the South Col. In this picture, the south face, partly shrouded in clouds, displays its impressive slopes, the product of the collision between the Indian tectonic plate and the Euroasiatic plate, which took place some forty to sixty million years ago. This collision gave rise to the highlands of Tibet and to the Himalayas, which - in the Tibetan tongue, Ima Laya - means "the Land of Snows". The Himalayan mountain system describes a gigantic arc sweeping for some 2500 kilometers in length, and nearly two hundred and fifty kilometers in width, and contains the thirty tallest mountains on the earth. Photograph by Toru Nakano / Agence Freestyle.

to the measurement of the Himalayan peaks and to the definition of the earth's size and shape. In recognition of his exceptional contribution to science and to exploration, in an era when every expedition meant overcoming unbelievable obstacles and difficulties, Everest's name was linked to the name of the highest mountain on the planet. During the same years, the first peaks higher than six thousand meters were scaled, not "because they were there," but in order to place trigonometric signals on the peaks. Between 1865 and 1885, the Survey of India organized campaigns for further study beyond the forbidden frontiers, making use of specially trained persons who disguised themselves as merchants, saints, or pilgrims. These remarkable individuals hid the notes concerning their travels inside their prayer wheels, in place of the scrolls with religious mantras. Thus, a few of them actually made their way around Everest as early as 1871, and others pushed as far as Mongolia, while others still demonstrated that the Tsang-po and the Brahmaputra were in reality two different stretches of the same watercourse. Only around 1882, with the expeditions of W. Graham, who was travelling in the company of the Swiss guide Joseph Imboden, did the peaks of the Himalayas begin to qualify as the destination for "sporting" climbs, similar to the sort of activity that had begun to be practiced in the Alps nearly a century earlier. The Himalayas thus began to exert a brand-new allure upon the men of the world.

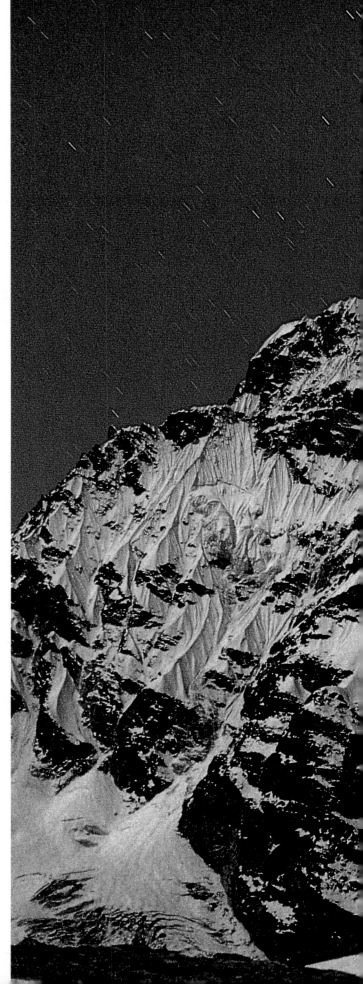

58-59 *Nightfall does nothing to diminish the grandeur of the Himalayas, which appear indeed even closer to the sky, the eternal abode of gods and dreams. In this picture, Chamlang, which rises to an altitude of 7290 meters in the Makalu region, in Nepal, is surrounded by surreal lights: these are stars which appear to be moving due to the extended exposure used in this shot. Photograph by Pat Morrow.*

59 top *The earliest light of dawn is reflected from the perennial glaciers and the immaculate snow - this is the remarkable show that nature stages every day on the slopes of Annapurna. Photograph by Pascal Tournaire.*

60-61 *The blues and greys of the final stretch of the glacier Ngozumpa, which emerges from Cho Oyu and drops down to flow into the Khumbu Valley in Nepal, harmonize perfectly with the white of the snowy slopes that stand above them. Photograph by Marco Majrani.*

62 Snow and ice, in perpetual motion on the high peaks of the Himalayas, create delicate and elegant formations. In this picture, it is possible to admire in detail the structures that cut deeply into the north face of Everest, usually called "organ pipes" or "wedding veils". Photograph by Greg Child.

63 The harmonious interplay of snow and wind confer a particular elegance to the slopes of Khumbutse, a splendid mountain in the group of Everest. Photograph by Pascal Tournaire.

64-65 The imposing structure of Gyachung Kang, a peak nearly eight thousand meters tall that lies at the mouth of the Gokyo Valley, in Nepal, shows the horizontal arrangement of the sedimentary strata that can be found in the original position. Photograph by Galen Rowell / Mountain Light.

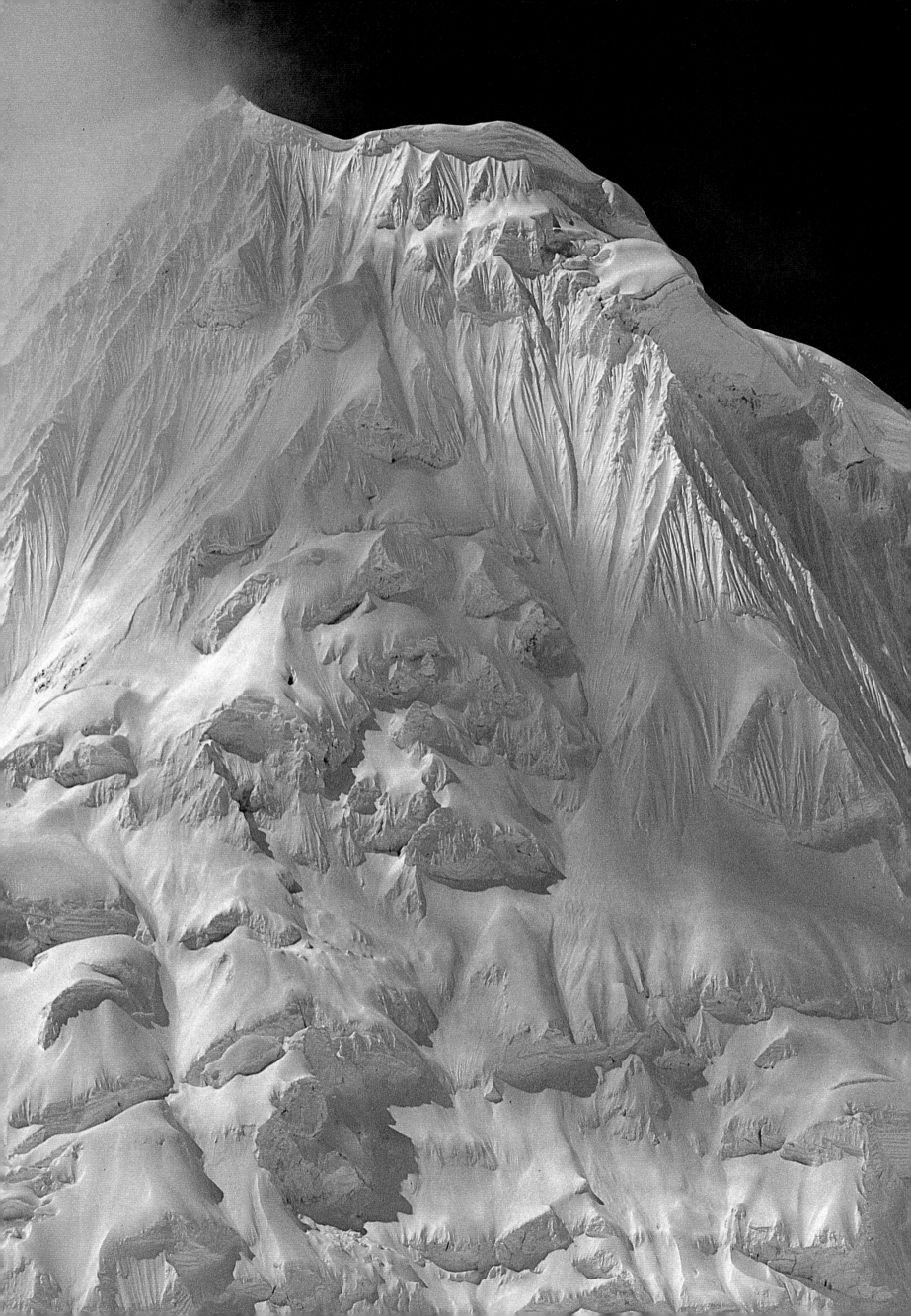

66   *The pyramidal shape of Pumori, 7145 meters, is perfectly regular and has an almost magical effect on all those who observe it. In fact it seems to grow gradually as one moves closer. This view of it, taken from the moraines of the Khumbu glacier, confirm the mountain's reputation as one of the most beautiful peaks in the world.*
Photograph by Christophe Boisvieux.

67 *In this picture, it is possible to observe the steep wall of Ama Dablam, a peak nearly six thousand meters tall that adorns the landscape of Nepal, again in the Khumbu region. The name of this mountain* *means "Necklace of the Mother", and in effect the hanging serac which can be seen just below the peak does look like a necklace at a woman's neck.* *Photograph by Christophe Boisvieux.*

68-69 *Daunting sheer cliffs and giant seracs adorned by ice are distinctive features of the south face of Annapurna, a mountain that towers 8091 meters above sea level. This treacherous wall constitutes one of the most difficult challenges in modern mountain* *climbing. During the hottest hours of the day, in fact, the eternal silence of the mountains is disturbed by the rumbling of immense avalanches, a sound that goes echoing through the valleys.* *Photograph by Pascal Tournaire.*

INDIA
THE MOUNTAINS OF PRAYER

*I*ndia possesses the largest portion of the Himalayan chain, practically the entire western section (the states of Jammu and Kashmir, Himachal Pradesh, Uttar Pradesh) and the far eastern section (Arunachal Pradesh), as well as the Darjeeling sector, located between Bhutan and Nepal. To all this we must add the tiny kingdom of Sikkim, which is a protectorate and the twenty-second State of the Indian Union. The kingdom of Bhutan is independent, but it too relies upon India for its foreign policy. The most interesting sections of the Indian Himalayas are Ladakh, which also includes Zanskar, the area around the source of the Ganges, in Uttar Pradesh, and Sikkim, with Kangchenjunga (8597 meters), the third tallest mountain on the planet. The western region has been for many years a bone of contention between India and Pakistan. Ever since 1949, there has been a de facto boundary between the two states, which runs just to the north of Srinagar and Leh, while the cease-fire line of 1962 and 1965 assigns to China Aksai Chin, the easternmost area of Ladakh. This situation, a product of the war between India and China and between India and Pakistan, is rejected by India, which claims the territories that have supposedly been taken from her. As a result of these border disputes, the only area that is actually open to tourism in the districts of Jammu and Kashmir is the zone south of Leh and east of Srinagar, while in the high valleys of Karakorum to the south of K2, a war of attrition is being fought, with frequent exchanges of cannon fire. Ladakh, the "Land of High Passes", is accessible from Srinagar along the ancient salt route, through the 3550 meter altitude of the historical Zoji-La, the "pass of the aspens", and the 4100 meter altitude of the Fotu-la. Today, Ladakh offers the most significant cross-section of Tibetan culture and architecture, far superior to what is available in the devastated Chinese-occupied Tibet. Ladakh, cradle of the origins of Lamaistic Buddhism, a philosophy that developed some two and a half centuries before Christ, is a world that is still locked into the Middle Ages, and which did not break its isolation from the West until 1974, after twenty-seven years of total embargo. The social structure that guides the life of the community is still typically feudal in nature, as is the architecture of the civic and religious buildings. The huge and spectacular statue of the Buddha Maitreya, the "Buddha of the Future", carved during the sixth century directly into the granite wall, marks a virtual gateway into the world of Lamaist Buddhism.

The most striking thing, as soon as one enters Ladakh and moves past the two high passes, is the remarkably clear and luminous air, joined to the sharp contrast between the bright white of the perennial snows which crown towering nameless peaks and the luxuriant green of the oases at the bottom of the valley, where the presence of fresh water from the runoff of the glaciers has made it possible to transform the harsh highland desert into an immense fruit orchard, where delicate apricots and cherries grow. The swift gallop of clouds across the sky rarely results in rain here. The deep clefts of the valley, devoid of vegetation, represent an ideal opportunity for geologists to engage in study and analysis. Along the trails, it is possible to admire a complete array of those "praying machines" about which we talk at some length in the introduction: mani walls with thousands and thousands of carved stones, stretching for as long as a kilometer or more in some cases, series of chorten, banners and prayer wheels spinning and fluttering in the winds or driven by the rushing waters of mountain streams. The forces of nature are here harnessed in the most passive of ways, in order to transform prayer into an unending flow that envelopes all things. The mani stones constitute an open-air art gallery: some of them denote an exceptional manual skill and fine gifts of expression on the part of the pilgrims that have worked on them, and all of them in any case serve as indicators of the correct and safest route to follow. The prayer wheels often have mechanisms that produce sound effects, extremely useful in case of fog, when the wayfarer can rely upon their tinkling and rattling sound to guide his footsteps.

In this region, there are some ten thousand monks; this means that one out of every nine persons is devoted to a life of religious practice and contemplation. Every family is proud to offer a child to the monkhood, in the secret hope that their offspring may one day prove to have the moral and personal traits worthy of a lama.

71 *This handsome closeup shows the severe, but at the same time, serene, gaze of a woman of Ladakh; perhaps it is precisely the silence of the "Land of Mountain Passes", which is what Ladakh means, that gives a special allure to the faces of the people that live there. This picture also allows us to admire in detail the ubiquitous headgear, made of astrakhan wool, and the* perak, *a strip of fabric encrusted with jewels and turquoises, which women wear at all times. Furthermore, gold and silver necklaces and earrings, with coral, turquoise, cornelian, and river pearls complete the outfit, offering some indication of the skill of the goldsmiths. Women, who enjoy the same rights as men, play an important role in this society where polyandry has been practiced for centuries; when women contract a marriage, they also marry their brothers-in-law.*
Photograph by Marcello Bertinetti.

The Tibetan term lama, *meaning "master", does not automatically refer to a monk: in truth, only a very few monks ever attain the rank of* lama. *Ladakh preserves a remarkable series of monastic centers that have maintained intact their architecture and original spirit: among the most important, let us mention Leh, the capital; the spectacular Tikse and Lamayuru; the ancient Alchi and Hemis; the remote Phuctal and Rangdum, in Zanskar. All of these monasteries are distinguished by their activity and by the religious ceremonies that take place in them, but the most important festival, which each year summons monks and pilgrims from all over the region, is that which is held in June of each year in Hemis, and which commemorates the birth of the first* Rimpoche, *the* lama *who directs the monastery. The ceremony involves the participation of a great many people, both lay and religious, who still wear traditional outfits. Women, in particular, show off their family jewels, among which the most important is the* perak, *a distinctive form of headgear made of astrakhan, upon which a long strip of cloth is fastened and studded with turquoise, coral, amber, agate, and silver. Nothing in the world could persuade a Tibetan woman to part with her* perak, *as it represents the dowry, received from her mother, which she will impart to her daughter. The wealthiest women also wear scarves and clothing of the finest* pashmina *wool, produced by the famous goats of the Kashmir. All the women wear silver reliquaries around their necks, in which rolled-up parchment scrolls bearing the sacred* mantras *are contained. The monastic centers, which are full-fledged villages, are run according to feudal regulations, and are entirely self-sufficient.*
The estates owned by the monastery are cultivated by the peasants, who pay tithes in "nature" to the monks. The monks, in exchange, govern the village, adminstering justice and settling whatever disputes may arise, providing spiritual and cultural advice, and also performing the job of teaching. There was a time when monastic complexes such as Lamayuru and Tikse housed hundreds of monks. Today, the numbers have dwindled but are still quite impressive.
At the center of the household economy of a Ladakh family is the yak, or Bos grunniens, *a large,*

partially domesticated bovine that is perfectly suited to life and work at high altitudes. Every part of the body of this animal is used, from the hide to the horns, the milk, the meat, the hooves, and the excrement, which serves as fuel in substitution of the rare and precious wood. The Ladakh house is devoid of fireplaces and has very small windows, so as to preserve heat during the chilly winters. The roof is covered with layers of bundle sticks that serve to insulate and keep in the heat. The region of Zanskar, the "Land of White Copper", which constitutes the most archaic and hard-to-reach part of Ladakh, remains isolated for almost eight months out of the year. But right in the heart of the winter, when the cold is particular harsh, contact is established once again between Padum and Lamayuru. Caravans move along the frozen waters of the Zanskar river, which temporarily receives a new name, Tchadar, or "frozen river".
The exceptional photographs by Olivier Föllmi that we shall see in the following pages tell the story of two young brothers who leave their village to go off to school at Leh, and who travel the difficult and dangerous icy route in order to go back to see their mother again after almost three years spent far away. The Garhwal region, in the west-central region of the Indian Himalayas, is one of the most sacred areas in the entire mountain chain, fulcrum of Hindu culture and religion.
The source of the Ganges, located at the base of the peaks of the Bhagirathi, the peaks of Nanda Devi and Shivling, the towns of Gangotri, Badrinath, and Kedarnath, are venerated both by Hindu pilgrims and by those of other religious persuasions. In the local symbology, the glaciers that descend from the mountains represent the white hair of Shiva. Among the faithful who climb to the source of the sacred river there are sadhus, *yogis, and other remarkable and enigmatic individuals, men who live according to ascetic rules, in absolute poverty. Despite the stinging cold of the four thousand meters of elevation, the* sadhus, *endowed with an exception control of their own bodies, remain almost entirely naked and sleep in the open each night, always immersed in prayer and in the most difficult of yogic exercises, without ever changing their rigid expressions.*

72 *This picture shows the kitchen area inside a typical house in Ladakh, where the residences are generally built without windows, with a view to the conservation of heat during the harsh winters; light penetrates only from above through a small skylight.*
Photograph by Didier Givois.

73 *A woman of Leh prepares the classic Tibetan tea, based on salted yak butter. Photograph by Earl Kowall.*

74-75 *This remarkable panoramic view allows us to admire the valley in which Leh, the capital of Ladakh, lies. Once this city was a fundamental stopping point on the lengthy Silk Road; today Leh, with a population of eleven thousand, has become the destination of international tourists. At the center of the photograph one can see the Queen's Palace framed amidst the prayer banners that entrust their messages of devotion to the winds. Photograph by Marcello Bertinetti.*

77 top *A group of monks from the sect of the "Yellow Hats", to which the Dalai Lama, the highest religious authority among Buddhists, belongs, participates in one of the ceremonies that are held each year in the monastery of Tikse. Photograph by Christophe Boisvieux.*

77 bottom *The monastery of Tikse, one of the most handsome and ancient in Ladakh, houses a hundred or so monks. The sacred complex, which lies amongst the mountains south of Leh, was built in the fifteenth century as the abode of spectral and protective demons. Photograph by Marco Majrani.*

76 *This splendid statue of Buddha, preserved in the monastery of Tikse, shows the skill of the Tibetans in the art of sculpture. They make use of a great variety of materials, including wood (shown here), bronze, and stone. At times, figurines are also made of more ephemeral materials, such as plaster, clay, and even butter and cheese! As for the preparation of statues in butter, there is even a school in Lhasa for aspiring "sculptors." The statues, which may be as tall as three meters, are shaped over a wooden or cardboard support that is wrapped in* tsampa, *a paste of toasted barley flour, butter, salt, ginger, and tea, all of which is then boiled in melted yak butter. The sacred rituals call for the monks to eat bits of these statues. Photograph by Christophe Boisvieux.*

Local mythology would have it that there are sadhus who live to be three or four hundred years old, dwelling in the highest mountain passes, never descending to the valleys where other men might see them, and nourishing themselves on rays of sunlight. A number of pilgrims go as high as 5500 meters to gather water and snow which they carry back to their homes. Many die of cold, hunger, or exhaustion during the climb; others simply "renounce life", detaching themselves materially from all earthly concerns, surviving only to cultivate their souls, while awaiting the death of their bodies. For Hindu pilgrims, to die near the source of the Ganges is considered to be a great privilege, much as the Buddhists consider anyone who is killed while making their way around the sacred mountain of Kailas to be extremely fortunate. Sikkim, Bhutan, and the Himalayas of Assam are the portions of the mountain chain where one is least likely to make the acquaintance of a western tourist. Sikkim shares the third-highest mountain in the planet with Nepal: the sacred Kangchenjunga, the "Five Strongboxes of the Great Snow". The few mountain climbers who have scaled the mountain have undertaken not to set foot on the peak, but to remain at least a few meters lower down, in order to keep from profaning the altar of the gods. Bhutan, or Druk-Yul in the Tibetan tongue, has only recently been opened to foreigners. This is a feudal kingdom that is rich in traditions and folklore. The sovereign has long denied permission to mountaineering expeditions to enter his country, until just a few years ago, and this has helped to create an aura of mystery over the mountains and valleys of Bhutan. The prevailing religion is Lamaist Buddhism, and the territory is rich in monasteries, especially in the area around Thimpu and Phunaka, respectively the summer and winter capitals. Of particular importance are the religious ceremonies, which are full of ancient and unusual rituals, with a remarkable display of costumes and an exceptionally complex set of symbolisms. Last of all, in the easternmost part of the Himalayas, where the Tsang-po/Brahmaputra follows a wide curve that leads down to the Bay of Bengal, we find Arunachal Pradesh. This is a zone visited by very few tourists indeed, not well known, and this is chiefly due to the

political complications that afflict the areas around the MacMahon Line, drawn in 1914 to mark the boundaries between India and China. In the westernmost portion of this area one finds the important Buddhist monastery of Tawang. Most of the peaks around this area have not yet been scaled, and only a very few expeditions have made any effort to climb these peaks. In any case, mountain climbers would be the first to recall that the great Indian poet, Kalidas, who lived between the fourth and fifth century B.C., considered the Himalayas to be a divine personification, worthy of adoration. This is how Kalidas began his poem Birth of the God of War, borrowing themes from the Vedic cantors dating from 1500-1200 B.C.: "To the north is the lord of the mountains, who is called Himalaya. He is of divine descent, he plants his roots in the two seas, to east and west, setting himself as a measure of the boundless Earth... From the depths of the earth you take your flight, oh Himalaya; the pride of your peaks and of your spirit are of the same essence."

78-79 In the monastery of Hemis, an ancient religious center in Ladakh, built at the beginning of the seventeenth century, a festival is held in the month of June, and the faithful come from all over Tibet and India to participate. This ritual, which involves a series of ceremonies and dances with profound meanings, is in honor of the birthday of the god Padmasambhava. During the course of the festival, which lasts for a number of days, the monks wear costumes and wooden masks and stage full-fledged theatrical performances which evoke episodes from the life of Buddha and the saints and portray the perennial conflict between Good and Evil.
Photographs by Giancarlo Zuin.

80-81 The monastery of Lamayuru, which dates from the tenth or eleventh century, and is the oldest in Ladakh, appears suddenly at the far end of the valley, perched upon a mountain, similar to a mighty fortress. Inside, the monastery offers remarkable surprises as well: many of the rooms are dug directly into the rock, and are decorated with frescoes and sculptures. In the monastery, moreover, there is an interesting library and a rather unusual statue that depicts a deity with eleven heads and a thousand arms.
Photograph by Christophe Boisvieux / Explorer.

82 left *Gangotri, in the Indian region of Uttar Pradesh, is the village closest to the sources of the Ganges, and it is the destination for an endless river of the Hindu faithful. In this photograph, one can admire the first temple dedicated to the "divine" Ganges. Photograph by Marcello Bertinetti.*

82 right *A* sadhu, *or holy man, is portrayed as he walks toward his humble abode, located in Gangotri. Legend has it that among the most inaccessible mountains, there are* sadhus *that live to be three or four hundred years old, feeding only on the rays of the sun. Photograph by Marcello Bertinetti.*

83 *The rocks that are carved and smoothed by the ever flowing waters of the Ganges, near Gangotri, are an ideal spot for the profound meditation of the sadhus. Photograph by Marcello Bertinetti.*

84 top *The three peaks of Bhagirati, near Gaumukh, rise not far from the source of the Ganges. In the foreground one can see a rock inscribed with sacred symbols and* mantras, *the distinctive prayerful invocations. Photograph by Marcello Bertinetti.*

84-85 *The* sadhu Swami *Balawan climbs barefoot over the glaciers that lead to the source of the Ganges. These holy men are extremely resistant to cold and to the most extreme environmental and climatic conditions. Photograph by Marcello Bertinetti.*

86-87 *After reaching Gaumukh, indicated as the site of the source of the Ganges, the* sadhu Swami *Balawan performs complex yoga exercises in which he shows that he has complete control over his body. The altitude is 4300 meters, and the temperature is several degrees below zero Celsius. Photograph by Marcello Bertinetti.*

88 *Another photograph of the* sadhu *Swami Balawan, in a position of devotion and prayer. True yoga masters, these ascetics spend their entire lives wrapped up in contemplation, prayer, and meditation. Photograph by Marcello Bertinetti.*

89 *The last rays of sunlight illuminate the peak of Shivling, a mountain that stands 6543 meters tall, and which is interesting not only because of the remarkable beauty of its slopes, but because of the sacred aura that surrounds it. The mountain's name links it to the deity Shiva, the most terrifying of all Hindu gods because Shiva destroys all things, whether evil or good, in order to make way for new creations. Shivling means* lingam *- or the phallus - of the god Shiva. This peak stands in the Indian Garhwal, a territory that is sacred as well because the river Ganges rises in the surrounding area. Photograph by Marcello Bertinetti.*

90 *An old man, photographed in front of his house in the heart of Zanskar, is deep in prayer; he holds a "prayer wheel" in his hands, one of the most distinctive and widespread tools of prayer. Photograph by Olivier Föllmi.*

91 *On the face of this aged woman, it is possible to see the marks of time. Wind, cold, and the sun that beats down on the impenetrable valleys of Zanskar have in fact profoundly cut and wrinkled her skin. In these regions, the average lifespan is sixty years, and very few people live longer than that. Infant mortality is fifty percent of all births, and a great many women still die during childbirth. Photograph by Olivier Föllmi.*

92-93 *This grandmother, in her seventies, tells a story to her little granddaughter. Inside the home, the temperature often barely reaches two degrees above zero Celsius. Heating is based on yak dung, which serves as a valuable source of fuel when burned. Tibetans protect their skin from the harsh climate by spreading a thick layer of yak butter upon themselves. Photograph by Olivier Föllmi.*

95 *A short procession of men moving in the earliest light of dawn through the Pensi pass, at an altitude of 4400 meters. In the spring, it becomes necessary to travel by night, when the temperature drops and the* snow becomes strong enough to support the weight of a human being; by day, when the temperature rises and the footing becomes dangerous and uncertain, one rests.
Photograph by Olivier Föllmi.

96-97 *The Zanskar river is partially iced over during the winter months, and it becomes a full-fledged footpath. Along this route, Motup, a thirteen-year-old boy, leaves the village where* *he lives with his parents and sister, and makes his way, along a dangerous route, to Leh, where he will be able to attend school.*
Photograph by Olivier Föllmi.

98-99 *In the dim light that penetrates the valley, Motup guides his little sister Diskit, just eight years old, along the treacherous icy surface with the help of a stick - even the slightest misstep in these conditions would be fatal.*
Photograph by Olivier Föllmi.

100-101 *The fragile sheets of ice constitute a mortal danger in the storm. Falling into the water at these temperatures, wearing heavy felt clothing, would mean being swept away by the rushing stream, and certain and rapid death.*
Photograph by Olivier Föllmi.

102 *A brief pause along the way allows the travellers to gather their strength with a hot cup of barley beverage. In order to make the trip along the Zanskar river, it is necessary to travel at dawn, when the biting cold offers the greatest assurance that the ice will hold.*
Photograph by Olivier Föllmi.

103 *At dawn, after drinking tea with yak butter, the travellers stretch their hands over the coals in order to enjoy a bit of warmth, and to get their blood circulating before starting off again.*
Photograph by Olivier Föllmi.

104-105 *When the river provides no sheets of ice upon which to walk, it becomes necessary to clamber along the slick walls that rise over the river. It is not difficult to understand why so many people die in the Himalayas while travelling from one village to another. Photograph by Olivier Föllmi.*

106-107 *This picture shows, once again, Motup as he proceeds cautiously along his route, making his way with the aid of a walking stick which helps him in keeping his balance on the slippery and treacherous rocks. Photograph by Olivier Föllmi.*

108 *This picture shows Diskit, Motup's younger sister, in a thoughtful pose. Within Tibetan society, women are held in great esteem, and in fact it is often the women that rule the family, in a form of matriarchy, particularly common in Ladakh. This is why it should surprise no one that many families make enormous sacrifices in order to give the daughters - as well as the sons - an excellent education.*
Photograph by Olivier Föllmi.

109 *Motup's intense gaze reveals the resilient soul of a young boy who has grown up early. There are very few children who travel from the heart of Zanskar all the way to Leh to study. Motup has been very fortunate, but he has fully repaid his parents for all of their sacrifices. At school, indeed, he has learned to read and write, he has studied the English language, and he has acquired a great many notions which will help him to improve the quality of life of his family, once he returns to the village.*
In the photograph below, Motup is shown with his fellow students in the courtyard of the school, which was inaugurated by the Dalai Lama in person, as is commemorated by the plaque in the distance.
Photographs by Olivier Föllmi.

NEPAL
THE VERTICAL LAND

110 top *The roofs of the temples of Durbar Square, in Patan, distinguish the valley of Kathmandu, in Nepal. At the center is a gold-covered statue of the king Malla, forefather to the Newari dynasty which ruled the country for centuries, during the Middle Ages. Photograph by Layma Yann / Explorer.*

110 bottom *A group of Buddhist monks gathers in a temple in Kathmandu. These monks form part of the sect - not reformed - of the "Red Hats", the oldest of all the religious congregations. Photograph by Marcello Bertinetti.*

A paragon of religious tolerance and peaceful cooperation amongst profoundly diverse ethnic groups, Nepal contains the best known section, the very "heart" of the Himalayan chain. No fewer than eight of the fourteen eight-thousand meter peaks of the planet lie in the 140,000 square kilometers of Nepal's territory. The mountain peaks of Nepal exert a powerful allure upon mountain climbers, but also upon simple tourists, who can enjoy a total immersion in an environment that, save for a very few exceptions, is no different now from the way it was several centuries ago. Nepal, governed since 1951 by a constitutional monarchy, encourages tourism and scientific research within its borders. In 1953, when Everest was first scaled, there were no paved roads in Nepal, and the capital, Kathmandu, could only be reached on foot or in a small airplane. The country has made noteworthy progress, making the best possible use of the natural beauty and artistic heritage that constitute its chief source of wealth. The creation of a full-fledged tourist industry has attained levels of reliability that may be unrivalled in any undeveloped nation. Nowadays, it is possible to travel freely and sightsee in this extremely interesting land, with the full support of local organizations, which rely chiefly on the assistance of very well prepared sherpa guides. Unlike what is commonly believed, "Sherpa" means neither "guide" nor "bearer"; rather it identifies members of a people, that lives in the region of Khumbu, a section of the slopes of Everest. Buddhist by religion, the Sherpas, "men of the East", have a particular vocation for mountain climbing, to the point that full-fledged schools have been established to prepare young Sherpas for careers as guides for trekking and for expeditions. Norgkay Tenzing, the man who first reached the peak of Everest together with Sir Edmund Hillary, belonged to this ethnic group. During expeditions, Sherpas carry only their own personal load, and they never serve as bearers, which is a task given to men and women from villages in the valley that is being explored or near the mountain that is to be climbed. The experience of a trip to Nepal is ideal as the first contact with the world of the Himalayas, because in Nepal it is possible to observe and study at the same time all of the situations that can be found in other parts of the mountain chain.

111 In this aerial view, we can admire the giant stupa of Boudnath, built in the fifth century in the valley of Kathmandu. Its five-story structure possesses a massive tower that stands forty meters high. The sanctuary represents an image of the Universe, and is an object of worship only to the Buddhists of Tibet. Its origins are shrouded in the mists of time, and legend has it that a woman named Kangma asked the king for a piece of land the size of a buffalo hide on which to build a temple in honor of the Amitabha Buddha. When the king agreed, the woman very cleverly cut the hide into a great many thin strips, tied them one to the other, and lay them on the ground, tracing the perimeter of the land on which the Boudnath now stands. Photograph by R. Ian Lloyd / First Light.

112 *A woman smokes tobacco, drawing intently on the traditional water pipe, which is decorated with the distinctive motifs of Nepalese culture. Photograph by Marcello Bertinetti.*

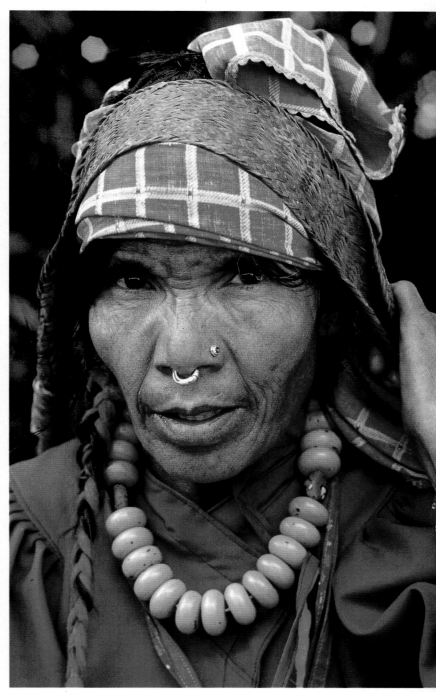

113 left *This photograph depicts a Rai bearer who lives at the foot of Everest. Nepal is a melting pot of races; in fact, there are some twenty different ethnic groups. Photograph by Pat Morrow/First Light.*

113 right *In the foreground, we see a Gurung woman, member of a people that live in the Marsyangdi Valley, near Annapurna. Photograph by Galen Rowell / Mountain Light.*

Nepal practically represents a summary of all the excitement of the Himalayas, a concentrate of all possible sensations. Here the Buddhist world and the Hindu world are equally represented, in the most spectacular manner possible. And such is the religious syncretism that it becomes perfectly normal for the faithful to enter and pray in a Hindu temple and then behave in the most perfectly Buddhist manner. A great many Nepalese say that they feel that they are at the same time believers in both religions. There may be no other place in the Himalayas where it is possible to admire such a concentration of cultural and artistic beauty. The valley of Kathmandu alone, center of the culture of the refined Newari people, who produced the dynasty that led to the unification of Nepal at the end of the eighteenth century, takes several weeks to tour in its entirety. Such centers as the capital, Kathmandu, or Patan, the ancient medieval city closely tied to the capital, or like Bhaktapur, Pashupatinath, and Nuwakot, are so rich in ancient religious and civil monuments that they constitute a unique opportunity for study or for contemplation, although the massive presence of tourists has somewhat diluted the allure and poetry that once hovered everywhere. The splendor of the ancient dynasties of feudal times, foremost among them the dynasty of the Malla, has managed to survive chiefly because Nepal has never been a theater of truly devastating wars, nor has it had to undergo domination on the part of hostile invaders. The temples of Swayambunath and Durbar Square, the giant and ancient stupa of Boudnath, the medieval palaces of Patan and Bhaktapur, all are monuments of considerable beauty and importance, the heritage of the entire world, as were the temples and palaces destroyed in Tibet. Alongside the image of modernization that Nepal offers its visitors, it should be pointed out however that even today the only way in which one can move from one place to another within the country is aboard the small touring aircraft and through the power of one's own legs. And they must be muscular legs, if one is to climb the slopes that lead up to the highest altitudes. The reward for all this effort is quite tangible: glittering and arrow-sharp peaks, jabbing into cobalt-colored skies; nights in which the light of the stars tinges the glaciers and the white faces of the mountains with a surreal bluish hue; deep, lush, green valleys; monasteries where contemplation verges still closer to the supernatural; villages rich in a humanity that is poor but decorous and dignified, with the greatest respect for the ancient traditions of the fathers; affable tribes that are always well intentioned toward foreign guests; rivers white with foam that rush giddily down toward the vast plains of the Terai and toward the Ganges Valley. And so, if we except a few isolated episodes, limited only to the capital city, there are no modern hotels with all the comforts of the late twentieth century, there are no facilities for skiing, there are no superhighways. Even in the cities, the means of transportation most commonly used is the bicycle. The network of roads is still very limited, and each year it is almost entirely erased by the monsoon rains. There are a great many valleys, still practically unknown, which can be reached only at the price of many weeks of trekking. These are regions such as Karnali and Dolpo, the land of the snow leopard, which constitute the northwesternmost areas of the country, where the religion of Bon still flourishes. Bon is a sort of animistic religion that can fairly be considered a precursor to Buddhism. And the regions of Karnali and Dolpo have only recently been opened to very small groups of scholars, in the context of a very intelligent policy implemented by the government, which hopes to make the impact of tourism in the areas with the most archaic cultures as gradual as possible, thus limiting the violence of the clash. The Dolpo region is difficult to reach, beginning with the valleys of the zone to the west of Dhaulagiri.

In order to enter the region from the south, it is necessary to cross three passes that tower above five thousand meters. The villages of the Dolpo region are poverty-stricken due to their total isolation. In fact, although they are part of the Nepalese state, these valleys already form part of the Tibetan watershed, and they cannot be reached from the Chinese side for political reasons. In this perfectly intact environment lives the beautiful snow leopard, the rarest and most aloof of all the world's big cats. National Geographic Magazine published a spectacular photographic essay and article on the snow leopard which was the product of an extensive research project.

In areas such as this, the rule of limited numbers is

115 Namche Bazaar, a prosperous market town where it is possible to find just about everything, from Tibetan handicrafts to modern mountaineering equipment, is made up of wooden two-storey buildings, and is the capital of the Sherpas. It once took weeks on foot to reach this place from Kathmandu, but now it is possible to fly small aircraft in to the nearby town of Lukla. Namche Bazaar, which features small and comfortable hotels, is one of the obligatory points of passage for the many climbers and tourists heading for the valleys of Everest.
Photograph by Pat Morrow.

116 top *In late autumn, in the monastery of Thyangboche, at the foot of Ama Dablam, a sacred mountain at a lower elevation than Everest, the festival of Mani Rimdu is celebrated for two days. The dancers have prepared for the event over the days previous, fasting and reciting* mantras, *the sacred syllables that Buddhists chant during meditation. The spectator is presented with images that range from the horrible to the cheerful, interspersed with fragments from the rituals of the ancient, pre-Buddhist religion of Bon. Photograph by Galen Rowell / Mountain Light.*

in force, so as to prevent excessive pressure from great numbers of foreign visitors in areas whose delicate economic and social equilibrium could not withstand traumatic alterations. For the same reason, there are very few visitors to the valleys bordering Sikkim, and it is virtually impossible to reach the tiny affiliated feudal kingdom of Mustang, with its mysterious fortified capital of Lo Mantang, a wedge of territory that juts into Tibet, perhaps one of the most backward places on the entire planet. In regions such as these, and especially in the Khumbu region, the legend of the yeti has long flourished, the mythical "snowman", which became extremely popular after the Englishman Eric Shipton published a series of excellent photographs of fresh footprints in 1952. Few of those who believe in the yeti know that the adjective "abominable", which so often accompanies the creature's name, is the result of a misunderstanding. In fact, the Tibetans call they yeti midre gang-mi. Midre *means "bear-man" or "snow-bear", and* gang-mi *means "man of the glaciers". The word* midre *was erroneously interpreted by member of one expedition, and translated with the English adjective "abominable". The name "abominable snowman" made its way into the literature and the language, and there it remains. In the Sherpa language, the group of Everest is also known as Mahalangur-Himal, a name which means "the Himalayas of the great apes", and this is just one more piece of evidence supporting the legend of the yeti. Nepal, too, possesses a great many sacred places. From the monasteries of Thyangboche (Khumbu) and Muktinath (Annapurna Himal) to the lakes of Gosainkund (Langtang), from the river of Baghmati to the unattainable peaks of Machapuchare, Gauri Shankar, Ama Dablam, and Kangchenjunga. Much of the most popular trekking has as a final destination these monuments, these sites, or these mountains.
The trip around Annapurna and trips to the "Sanctuary", the horseshoe-shaped valley over which the south face of the mountain soars, and trekking to the base camp of Everest are some of the most popular trips that afford a first contact with the local environment.
Any visit to Annapurna and to the land of the Gurung people begins in the city of Pokhara, the

116-117 *The monastery of Thyangboche, shown here shrouded in the mists that envelope the sacred forest, stands on a steep ridge at an altitude of almost four thousand meters. Considered the most important center of Buddhism in the Khumbu region, in Nepal, it enjoys a splendid location, surrounded by peaks such as Everest, Lhotse, and Ama Dablam. Photograph by Albert Gruber.*

118-119 *In this picture, it is possible to admire part of the festival of Mani Rimdu, celebrated in the monastery of Jiwong. The monks attempt to acquire religious merit through the performance of dramas and dances in costume. These ceremonies are open to anyone who wants to take part in them, to whatever religious persuasion they may belong. Photograph by Christophe Boisvieux.*

second largest in Nepal. From the first foothills just to the north of town, the view of the Machapuchare, the "Matterhorn of the Himalayas", fully justifies its claim to the title of the most beautiful mountain in the world. Standing six thousand meters tall, Machapuchare, whose name means "Fishtail", because of the twin peaks, one alongside the other, and pounded by the winds, seems to "dangle" from the sky, floating in the haze. At dawn and at dusk, the peak takes on the most improbable colorations. A sacred mountain par excellence, the abode of the gods, Machapuchare has never been scaled because the authorities have refused to issue permits for the climb. In 1957, authorization was issued to an English expedition, on the understanding that the climbers halt at least fifty meters beneath the peak, in order to keep the mountain from being defiled, a condition which was respected under the vigilant eyes of the people from the surrounding villages. As one enters and climbs the Valley of Modi Khola, which is arguably the deepest valley in the world, set as it is amongst mountains of over six thousand meters whose peaks, on the opposite sides of the valley rift, are only a few kilometers apart as the crow flies, one can see the progressive development of the flora with the increase in altitude: from the rice paddies and other types of crops and plants typical of low-lying valleys, irrigated by ingenious systems of channels and streams, to the ficus forests and giant rhododendra of higher altitudes, all the way up to the conifers and finally the bamboo groves and steppes of the highlands. The flowers and other allied forms of vegetation which on the Alps are found at altitudes of two thousand meters, develop a good fifteen hundred meters higher up here, with species of flowers that are different though related biologically. In Nepal, naturalists can find endless sources of interest, but even those who are simply fond of nature and wilderness will be entranced by a sort of rapture of love that will never disappear, lasting the rest of their life. Along the mule trails, it is common to encounter endless caravans of mules carrying rice into Tibet, and returning with loads of rock salt, mute testimony to the lasting traditions of trade dating from the Middle Ages. When one reaches the "Sanctuary", one immediately understands the

120-121 This village stands in the land of the Sherpas, the Khumbu region, at about 3000 meters altitude. The houses are oriented in such a way as to receive the greatest amount of sunlight, which is one of the prime sources of heating for the inhabitants. With respect to those of Tibet and Ladakh, the windows are much larger. Here, indeed, the climate is less harsh, vegetation is luxuriant, and wood can be burnt as a fuel, while in drier and more arid regions, wood is too rare and precious to be burnt.
Photograph by Christophe Boisvieux.

121 top Two women bearers accompany a group of sightseers in Solo-Khumbu, the region around Everest. The weight of their load - some thirty kilograms - is borne entirely upon their head and neck. The shoulder-mounts are used only for balance.
Photograph by Pat Morrow.

reason for the name. A valley twelve kilometers in breadth, surrounded by peaks reaching from seven to eight thousand meters above sea level, enormous glaciers and drifting moraines, a continuous road of avalanches and collapsing seracs, tall as skyscrapers in Manhattan, and the four thousand meters of sheer vertical cliff face of Annapurna.

A similar spectacle awaits the visitors who make their way to the foot of Everest: the jagged series of seracs of the ice fall drops down amongst the tallest mountain on earth, Lhotse, and the sharp-tipped Nuptse. Further back is the perfect pyramid of Pumori, which dominates the immense flowing slab of the glacier Khumbu. Today, at the base camp of Everest there is the highest permanent laboratory for the study of human behavior at altitude, the famous "pyramid" erected by Ardito Desio, the organizer of the expedition that in 1954 brought Italian mountain climbers to the peak of K2, the second highest mountain on the planet.

A view of Everest is rather disappointing, but only because it is so closely packed in amongst other dizzying peaks, and so it is difficult to perceive its true height.

The best point of observation, which can be reached fairly easily as long as one is in training and is well acclimated, is the peak of Kala Pattar, about 5500 meters in altitude.

From this ideal balcony, it is possible to look out over one of the handsomest and most satisfying landscapes of the Himalayas.

Nepal, melting pot of races and contradictions, though probably only from the point of view of Westerners, impresses the soul with unforgettable sensations.

Time spent in contact with its strong and simple people gives one renewed vigor and offers a new philosophy in dealing with everyday life.

Along with one's memories, there is the desire to return to the Himalayas as soon as possible, to the land where mountains seem to float in the sky.

The path that must be trod in order to enjoy these visions is long and tiring, but let us remember what the master Aiareya Brahmana says:

"The heels of the traveller are like flowers.

His body grows and yields fruit. All of his sins disappear during the voyage."

122 *The city of Lo Mantang is the capital of the autonomous kingdom of the Mustang, in northern Nepal. This remote territory is inhabited by some six thousand individuals, distributed in far-flung villages surrounded by vast and arid desert* regions. *These communities still live in the depths of the Middle Ages, with very limited contact with outsiders; only a very few Westerners, in fact, have ever visited these remote areas.*
Photograph by Galen Rowell / Mountain Light.

123 *A chorten, a small Buddhist temple typical of mountainous territories, whose architecture symbolizes the Universe, rises against the clear skies of Lo Mantang, in the kingdom of the Mustang. Here society is still strictly broken down into castes, and many of the inhabitants still practice the ancient pre-Buddhistic religion of Bon, an extremely archaic Shamanistic and animist creed, which lives on only in the most distant and isolated regions of the Himalayas.*
Photograph by Galen Rowell / Mountain Light.

TIBET
THE INVISIBLE PATHS
OF THE SOUL

The great "province of Tebet," as Marco Polo described it, includes the entire vast and arid territory of the highlands, crisscrossed by countless mountainous formations, which pushes from the northernmost slopes of the Himalayas down into the heart of the Asian landmass. It covers more land area than all of Europe, much of it has yet to be explored, and it is inhabited by only six million genuine Tibetans, many of whom lead nomadic lives. The geological events that led to the lifting of this enormous tableland to an average altitude of 4500 meters are the same that led to the creation of the mountain chain. The geographic boundaries of the Himalayas reach all the way to the course of the Indus and the Tsang-po, but all the same our treatise includes a band to the north of this ideal demarcation line. In effect, we have attempted to provide an exhaustive description of the cultures of the Himalayas, and in so doing one can hardly ignore the historical and moral capital of the region, the city of Lhasa, although it actually lies some fifty kilometers to the north of the Tsang-po valley. All of Tibet, or Bodyul as it is called in the local tongue, rigorously follows the dicates of the Buddhist-Lamaistic credo. The Tibetan culture, then, also extends its influence to the Chinese regions of Qinghai, Gansu, Swechuan, Yunnan and Hinjiang, and to the western sectors of the Himalayas (Ladakh), to Bhutan, and to the high northern valleys of Nepal (Dolpo, Mustang, and Khumbu, the region of the Sherpas), and to Sikkim. The flight southward of many dozens of thousands of Tibetans, under the onslaught of Chinese aggression, has contributed to the further spread of this culture beyond the confines of Tibet. Forty-five years of Chinese occupation and the blind and destructive fury of the Red Guard under Mao, have caused incalculable damage, but these trials have not been sufficient to extinguish the religious sense of the Tibetans, although the Dalai Lama, the highest religious authority in Tibet, who was awarded the Nobel Peace Prize in 1989, was forced to flee, seeking haven in Dharamsala, in India. Despite the absolute prohibition against the practice of any religious observances whatsoever, imposed by the invaders, on pain of death, and despite the almost total destruction of the monasteries, of the stupas, of the chortens, and of the mani walls, which have all been banned as "hated symbols of feudalism and Lamaism", the tide of mystical beliefs and the culture of Lamaistic Buddhism has not been stemmed at all, and is now rising once again, ineluctable, and there have even been moments of bloody revolt, as in 1959, when eighty-six thousand persons were killed and a hundred thousand fled, or as in 1987. The Chinese authorities have changed their general attitude, and they are now working to rebuild and to save what can be salvaged, but immense historical and artistic treasures have been lost forever. According to one study, of the six thousand monasteries that existed in Tibet before 1959, only forty-eight have escaped any major damage in the period between 1966 and 1976, during the period of "democratic reforms" and the "Cultural Revolution", while the vast majority of the monasteries has been systematically leveled. The monks, who numbered 110,000 prior to the Chinese occupation, are now only fifteen hundred in number. Suffice it to compare a photograph of Gyantse now with a photograph of how it looked before, when it housed no fewer than ten thousand monks in an orderly cascade of buildings, clambering up the mountain, with a spectacular visual effect. Or else, suffice it to observe the skyline of the city of Lhasa, today glittering with undulating sheet metal, and once a great monastery qua city, were even the immense palace of Potala, the "Vatican of the Buddhists", thirteen floors tall and containing more than a thousand rooms, has been stripped of most of its superstructure and decorations, and despoiled of its art treasures and priceless libraries. The monasteries of Jokhang, Sera and Drepung, in the area around the capital, where the Red Guard camped for years, give us some idea of the proportions of the damage inflicted: the Red Guard burned the precious furniture, books, and thangkas, and besmeared the walls that artists had worked for centuries to decorate so beautifully. Perhaps the monastery of Ganden, founded in 1409, and which once housed five thousand monks of the sect of the "Yellow Hats", is the most emblematic victim of the disaster. Not one stone remains atop another, save for the few buildings rebuilt from scratch thanks to the contributions of private benefactors.

125 *A pilgrim praying alongside a* mani *wall by the banks of the river Tsang-po, in western Tibet. Mani walls are long bastions formed of stones that are generally carried from mountainous regions, and carved or sculpted by the faithful with depictions of sacred scenes or* mantras. *Photograph by Galen Rowell / Mountain Light.*

126-127 *Between 1949 and 1950, following the invasion of Tibet, the Liberation Army of the People's Republic of China began a full-fledged campaign of genocide. Mao's Red Guard was particularly savage in its treatment of the symbols of Buddhism and the six thousand monasteries then scattered across the land, of which only about fifty survive. In this panoramic view of the monastery of Ganden, not far from Lhasa, it is possible to see all too clearly the signs of violence and destruction. Prior to the invasion, the monastery, which stands at an altitude of four thousand meters, and which is certainly one of the houses of prayer that stands closest to the heavens, was home to five thousand monks. In this center of resistance to Chinese brutality and of support for Tibetan independence, today there live only three hundred monks, dwelling in the few buildings that have recently been reconstructed. Photograph by Galen Rowell / Mountain Light.*

128-129 *Lhasa, the city of the gods, is situated at an elevation of greater than 3600 meters in the Kyichu valley in Tibet. The city was divided into two parts after the Chinese invasion: the Tibetan quarter, the old city center distinguished by two- and three-storey houses and narrow streets, and the Chinese quarter, which sprang up at the foot of the Potala palace. This building, as can be seen in the photographs, has a facade that extends for four hundred meters, is thirteen storeys tall, and contains one thousand rooms, which in turn contain ten thousand altars and two hundred thousand statues. It was built in 1643, at the behest of the Dalai Lama, the "Pope" of the Buddhists, and served as the Dalai Lama's headquarters until 1959. Now, partially despoiled by the Chinese invaders, the palace awaits the return of its legitimate resident, the fourteenth Dalai Lama Tienzin Gyatso, the Nobel Peace Laureate in 1989, now in exile in Dharamsala, in India. Photographs by Giancarlo Zuin.*

130-131 *This photograph allows one to admire in detail the lavish decorations of the statue made of gilt wood which depicts the Buddha Maitreya, the "Buddha of the Future", and is located in the monastery of Jokhang. This monastery, the cathedral of Lhasa, is the destination of great crowds of pilgrims, who flock here from dawn till dusk. In the areas surrounding the city, which is the capital of Tibet, one can visit several of the very few monasteries which have been restored, in the wake of the devastation and vandalism perpetrated during the Cultural Revolution. Photograph by Albert Gruber.*

Out of the 108 buildings that once made up the monastery of Samye, the most ancient monastery in Tibet, built in A.D. 770, only the ground floor of the main building survives. The cynical genocide - both cultural and physical - that was perpetrated in Tibet, where one million two hundred thousand individuals were killed, according to the authorities in exile, over a sixth of the total population, is one of the worst crimes against humanity ever committed. In the Sixties and Seventies, while many "intellectuals" in the Western world praised the Maoist road to development, the silent and chilly highlands of Tibet were witnessing the most vile desecration of their centuries-long peace, to the absolute indifference of the world at large. It is our fondest wish that the remarkable stamina and resiliency of the Tibetans will make it possible for the process of artistic and cultural restoration and recovery to be completed, now that the Chinese authorities are willing to accept this, or at least no longer to oppose it as they did before. By now, in Tibet, an "autonomous region" in the framework of the People's Republic of China, there are seven million Chinese colonists side by side with the six million Tibetans. The process of assimilation of territory and of constant "ethnic cleansing" is probably irreversible; moreover, the Chinese have transformed the traditionally peaceful land of Tibet into a sort of giant landlocked aircraft carrier jutting down toward the Indian subcontinent. More than three hundred thousand armed men, seventeen radar stations, five missile bases, factories for the production of nuclear weapons, slagheaps of radioactive waste, and six landing strips for military jet fighters offer a complete picture of the current level of militarization of the territory. This disturbing information should not kill all hope, however. Despite the wounds that the land has suffered, Tibet still offers a visitor an amazing array of sights, alluring and beautiful, and the direct contact with the gentle and smiling Tibetan people, in whose eyes it is possible to glimpse an unsettling sadness, is still an enriching experience. The traditional hospitable offering of tea with the addition of salted butter made from yak milk should not be spurned, though it may be difficult for Western palates to become accustomed to such a singular taste, because the ritual of three cups of

131

tea still serves to create a bond of friendship.
In order to give some idea of the philosophy of these peoples, full of altruistic attitudes, let us quote one of their sayings: "May all beings, without exception, generate in their own minds the cause of serenity. If I manage to caress peace in my mind, let me be capable of conveying it to all other creatures. Let compassion and love be born where they have yet to grow, and there where they have bloomed, let them grow still more without limits." When one reaches Lhasa, the mysterious capital perched at an altitude of 3700 meters, the thin air, the pure skies, and the mystical aura that envelopes everything leaves an imprint in the soul that is not easy to forget. The grandeur of nature, which is largely uncontaminated here, offers unforgettable views of mountains glittering with snow and deep valleys, rivers crossed by tiny rope bridges, and old and dusty caravan tracks, where long lines of yaks still traverse. The only entirely Tibetan "8000" is Shishapingma, the "Crest over the Meadows", also known as Gosainthan, "Place of Saints", while Everest, Lhotse, Makalu, Manaslu, and Cho Oyu are shared with Nepal. Tibet does boast what well may be the most sacred area in the entire Himalayan region, the place where two great rivers have their sources, the Indus and the Tsang-po (which later becomes the Brahmaputra), Mount Kailas - Kailasa in Sanskrit - an imposing pyramid that soars to a height of 6700 meters, and which can be seen from an enormous distance as an incredibly pure crystal set in a sapphire sky. For Lamaistic Buddhists, for Hindus, and for the followers of the ancient religion of Bon, whose ancient origins predate Buddhism, Kailas is the "Father of the World", the fulcrum of the universe, and the place of the gods par excellence. Pilgrims make a long trek around the mountain, dozens of kilometers of difficult trail, tough and challenging, at altitudes of up to 5400 meters. Very few manage to make the whole trip in just twenty-four hours, most pilgrims take four or five days. Many die of exhaustion, cold, and dehydration; their bodies are abandoned where they collapsed, so that they can become "part of the Mountain". Like the Hindus at the source of the Ganges, faithful Buddhists think that to die here is to attain the peak of ecstasy. A number of pilgrims make the entire trip on their

132 In one of the courtyards of the monastery of Jokhang, in Lhasa, a woman burns aromatic herbs, following an ancient ritual which is accompanied by formulaic prayers.
Photograph by Didier Givois.

133 This picture captures the smile of a pilgrim in the monastery of Jokhang. After the last general uprising in 1987, the Chinese authorities recognized the futility of trying to eradicate with armed force the religious devotion of the Tibetans; the temples of Lhasa, therefore, have become once again the destination of pilgrims who come from everywhere in the Himalayan region.
Photograph by Ron Watts / First Light.

knees, or prostrating themselves at every step, turning their khor-lo, or portable prayer-wheels, the whole time. The recital of mantras - religious formulas or spells - is incessant; there are mantras for every occasion, for eating, for working, and even while defecating. Through meditation and prayer, the divine takes its place within humans. In this way, the pilgrims take weeks and even months to complete their journey, but for these people time does not have the same meaning that it does for us westerners. The faithful of the ancient creed of Bon, still fairly common in the region, as it is in the Nepalese regions of Mustang and Dolpo, make the trip around the mountain counterclockwise. All of the faithful of the other religions, on the other hand, travel around the mountain in a clockwise direction, as if they were moving around a chorten. Kailas is a sacred and inviolable mountain, but in 1985, the religious authorities of Tibet, in consideration of the great achievements of Reinhold Messner, gave the climber permission to scale Kailas in 1987. Messner surveyed the territory, but during this trip, his imagination was captured by the surreal beauty and spirituality of the place, and in accordance with his own conception of mountain climbing and his profound respect for the religion of the Tibetans, he decided not to climb Kailas, and gave up that possibility for ever, declaring that it was far more important to understand the mountain than to conquer it. And we can only be grateful to Messner for his contribution to preserving one of the last magical spots left on the planet, one of the last sources of romantic poeticism. Just a few miles away from Kailas, at an altitude of 4500 meters, is the pure and enchanted lake of Manasarovar, the "Mother of the World." Sacred to the Hindus, who believe that it is made up of the soul of Brahma, this lake too is the destination of pilgrimages made by many of the faithful. A great many of these pilgrims make their way around the entire lake - a good seventy kilometers - at a dead run, matching the rhythm of their run to the pace of their prayers. Every time that they take a breath, they recite the mantra "So' Ham", which literally translates as "I am that". The phrase indicates the substantial equivalence of Man and God, and happens to coincide with the sounds emitted while breathing, specifically while inhaling (So) and exhaling (Ham). On average, a human being will

134-135 *A nomadic family gathers under their yak-skin tent in Pekhu Tso, in western Tibet. The nomadic way of life is still widely practiced and the family groups move with their caravans of yaks and camels. Their sources of wealth are based on trade in rock salt and rice, precious stones and metals. Photograph by Galen Rowell / Mountain Light.*

135 top *In this picture, it is possible to admire the well-lit ground floor of the home of a smiling couple. In the Himalayan region, ethnic influences have been numerous and diverse, since ancient times, and so every face offers interesting surprises. Photograph by Pierre Toutain / Grazia Neri.*

repeat the mantra *"So' Ham"* about twenty thousand times a day: *every breath therefore reminds a human being: "I am He"*. The Nepalese greeting Namasté *means "I bow before the divinity that is present in you"*. *The inclination to create similarities between biological rhythms and prayer has a beneficent and relaxing effect upon the body. Modern techniques of biofeedback training are not very different from these ancient principles. Paradoxically, the Chinese invasion, instead of causing the disappearance of a culture, led the Tibetans to end their centuries of isolation, and to travel the world as exiles, spreading the profound underlying culture of their religion as well as familiarizing the rest of the world with their vast body of literature, the craftsmanship of their wool products and their carpets, their goldsmithery, their painting and poetry, and their science, which attained its highest levels in the fields of medicine and pharmacology. Ancient studies in human anatomy and on the relationship between the psyche and the body can be considered to underlie modern psychosomatic medicine, which is a newly acquired field of study for Western medicine, and is one of the foundation stones for the medicine of these highlands, which tends to concentrate on the causes of disease and illness, rather than on the symptoms. Over recent years, Tibetan cultural centers have sprung up everywhere. The art, which is essentially based upon religious motifs, is often unjustly criticized as repetitive. In reality, Tibetan art is no less varied than Byzantine art,*

and the artists have created an infinite array of variants upon a few basic motifs, showing particular gifts for miniatures, geometric balances, and the accentuation of motion which have few rivals. The extreme liveliness of the colors gives the works an exceptional intensity of expression. The selection of the new Dalai Lama is the most remarkable ritual of succession known. Indeed, the new Dalai Lama is not chosen through a conclave of the highest religious authorities in the land, but rather by searching among the young children of Tibet. The Dalai Lama is considered to be the reincarnation of the spirit of the first bodhisattva, *Avalokitesvara, the spiritual father and protector of Tibet. Forty-five days after the death of their spiritual leader, a delegation of monks is sent out around the land in search of the child that has displayed signs of a supernatural origin ever since birth. All Tibet is searched through and through, as far as the most remote valley and the farthest-flung village, a task that can take months or years. After working their way through a first set of candidates, the monks subject the children to an incredible series of tests and examinations. The future Dalai Lama must prove that he has a total familiarity with objects and places that he has never seen, since he must have become familiar with them during a previous incarnation, since his body is little more than "a piece of clothing that is put on and taken off". It seems incredible, and yet each time the miracle repeats itself.*

137 *A young woman, in the shelter of her tent, is preparing yak butter with the characteristic elongated churn. Yak butter is the foundation of the diet of all Tibetans, and it is also used as a cosmetic, to prevent the skin from drying out. The yak is a fundamental resource for those living in these mountains, not only because it is a sturdy means of transportation, but also because it provides milk and hides, from which clothing, blankets, and tents are made; the dung, lastly, is used as a fuel for heating. Photograph by Galen Rowell / Mountain Light.*

138-139 *A rudimentary boat made of animal hides sails along the Tsang-po river, near Lhasa. This great waterway marks the northern border of the Himalayan region. Photograph by Earl Kowall.*

140-141 *A caravan surrounded by yak-hide tents is encamped on the shores of Lake Rakas Tal. In the background, Mount Kailas rises impressively, the sacred mountain par excellence, the home of the deities Shiva and Parvati. Photograph by Pat Morrow.*

141 top *Pale clouds lap at the slopes of Gurla Mandata, one of the mountains sacred to Buddhists, which rises, in Western Tibet, to an altitude of 7728 meters. Photograph by Albert Gruber.*

142-143 *The monastery of Chiu rises near Lake Manasarovar. In this picture, the magical and imposing shape of Kailas, a mountain that the people of the Himalayas consider to be the Center of the* Universe *serves as a backdrop. Walking around Kailas for a Buddhist has much the same meaning as a pilgrimage to Mecca does for a Muslim. Photograph by Pat Morrow.*

144 *The eyes painted onto the tower of the stupa of the monastery of Swayambunath in Kathmandu symbolize the vigilance of the deity over human beings. Photograph by Marcello Bertinetti.*